REALITY THERAPY

A NEW APPROACH TO PSYCHIATRY

by

WILLIAM GLASSER, M.D.

With a Foreword by O. H. MOWRER, Ph. D.

PERENNIAL LIBRARY

Harper & Row, Publishers, New York
Grand Rapids, Philade
London, Singapo

D0124692

To G. L. Harrington, M.D.

A hardcover edition of this book is published by Harper & Row, Publishers, Inc.

First PERENNIAL LIBRARY ed

ISBN: 0-06-090414-3

15 16 17 18 RRD C 70 69 68 67 66 65 64 63

Contents

Foreword by O. Hobart Mowrer   vii

Acknowledgments   xix

Note to the Paperback Edition   xxi

PART I   THEORY

Introduction   3

1. Basic Concepts of Reality Therapy   5

2. The Differences between Reality Therapy and Conventional Therapy   42

PART II   PRACTICE

Introduction   63

3. The Treatment of Seriously Delinquent Adolescent Girls   67

4. Hospital Treatment of Psychotic Patients   107

5. The Office Practice of Reality Therapy   134

6. The Application of Reality Therapy to the Public Schools—Mental Hygiene   154

Foreword

This is an extraordinarily significant book. Readers will themselves discover that it is courageous, unconventional, and challenging. And future developments will, I predict, show that it is also scientifically and humanly sound.

For more than a decade now, it has been evident that something is seriously amiss in contemporary psychiatry and clinical psychology. Under the sway of Freudian psychoanalysis, these disciplines have not validated themselves either diagnostically or therapeutically. Their practitioners, as persons, have not manifested any exceptional grasp on the virtues and strengths they purportedly help others to acquire. And the impact of their philosophy of life and conception of man in society as a whole has been subtly subversive.

Because they were the main "losers," laymen were the first to become vocal in their discontent, distrust, and cynicism. But today there is a "shaking of the foundations" in professional circles as well. For example, a state hospital superintendent recently said to me: "Yes, we too think we have a good hospital here. At least we aren't doing the patients any harm. And that's progress. In the past, we psychiatrists have often *spread* the disease we were supposedly treating."

Late in his training as a psychiatric resident, Dr. Glasser saw the futility of classical psychoanalytic procedures and began to experiment with a very different therapeutic approach, which he eventually named Reality Therapy. Rather than a mere modification or variant of Freudian analysis, this system is in many ways absolutely antithetical. At the outset of Chapter 2, six postulates are listed as characterizing most forms of professional psychotherapy now practiced in the United States and Canada, ranging from "simple counseling through nondirective therapy to orthodox psychoanalysis." These six postulates or presuppositions are: the reality of mental illness, reconstructive exploration of the patient's past, transference, an "unconscious" which must be plumbed, interpretation rather than evaluation of behavior, and change through insight and permissiveness. The extent of Dr. Glasser's break with this total tradition is indicated by the following simple but bold statement: "Reality Therapy, in both theory and practice, challenges the validity of each of these basic beliefs." Moreover, Dr. Glasser states that the "conventional therapist is taught to remain as impersonal and objective as possible and not to become involved with the patient as a separate and important person" in a patient's life. In Reality Therapy, the helping person becomes both involved with and very real to the patient in a way which would be regarded as utterly destructive of the transference as conceived and cultivated in classical analysis.

More concretely and positively, what then *is* Reality Therapy? Chapter 1 answers this question, in concise and nontechnical language; and Chapters 3 to 6 exemplify the approach as it has been applied in various contexts. In essence, it depends upon what might be called a psychiatric version of the three R's, namely, *reality, responsibility, and right-and-wrong.*

Dr. Glasser begins at the end of this formula and asks, early in Chapter 1: "What is wrong with those who need psychiatric treatment?" The answer is that they have not been satisfying their *needs.* Here it might appear that Reality Therapy and psychoanalysis have something in common, but not so. For Freud, the needs which are presumably unfulfilled, in the so-called neurotic, are those of sex and aggression. For Glasser the basic human needs are for *relatedness* and *respect.* And how does one satisfy these needs? By doing what is realistic, responsible, right.

Granted that it is not always clear precisely *what* is right and what is wrong, Dr. Glasser nevertheless holds that the ethical issue cannot be ignored. He says:

To be worthwhile we must maintain a satisfactory standard of behavior. To do so we must learn to correct ourselves when we do wrong and to credit ourselves when we do right. If we do not evaluate our own behavior or, having evaluated it, if we do not act to improve our conduct where it is below our standards, we will not fulfill our needs to be worthwhile and will suffer as acutely as when we fail to love or be loved. Morals, standards, values, or right and wrong behavior are all intimately related to the fulfillment of our needs for self-worth and [are] . . . a necessary part of Reality Therapy.

Conventional psychiatry and clinical psychology assume that neurosis arises because the afflicted individual's moral standards are unrealistically high, that he has not been "bad" but *too good,* and that the therapeutic task is, specifically, to counteract and neutralize conscience, "soften" the demands of a presumably too severe superego, and thus *free* the person from inhibitions and "blocks" which stand in the way of normal gratification of his "instincts." The purview of Reality Therapy is, again, very different, namely, that human beings get into emotional binds, not because their standards are too high, but because their performance has been, and is, too low. As Walter Huston Clark has neatly put it, the objective of this (radically non-Freudian) type of therapy is not to lower the aim, but to increase the accomplishment. Freud held that psychological disorders arise when there has been a "cultural" interference with the instinctual, *biological* needs of the individual, whereas Glasser and others are now holding that the problem is rather an incapacity or failure at the interpersonal, *social* level of human functioning.

This categorical reversal of both the theory of neurosis and the intent of psychotherapy has far-flung implications. Freudian therapists and theorists concede, of course, that not everyone suffers from over-development of the superego. At least certain kinds of delinquents and criminals, they admit, have too little rather than too much conscience; and in the case of the very young and inexperienced, their problem is similarly a deficit of character rather than a presumed excess. Thus, in the psychoanalytic frame of reference, two types of "therapy" are called for, the one essentially educative, the other re-educative or "corrective" in the sense of *undoing* the effects of past efforts at socialization which have pre-sumably been "too successful." Dr. Glasser's view of the matter is quite different. He assumes that so-called neurotic and psychotic persons also suffer (although not so severely as do delinquents and frank sociopaths) from character and conduct deficiencies; and if this be the case, then all therapy is in one direction, that is, toward greater maturity, conscientiousness, responsibility. Glasser says:

> Using Reality Therapy, there is no essential difference in the treatment of various psychiatric problems. As will be explained in later chapters, the treatment of psychotic veterans is almost ex-actly the same as the treatment of delinquent adolescent girls. The particular manifestation of irresponsibility (the diagnosis) has little relationship to the treatment. From our standpoint, all that needs to be diagnosed, no matter with what behavior he expresses it, is whether the patient is suffering from irresponsibility or from an organic illness.

Not only does this author assume that all "psychiatric prob-lems" are alike; he also regards their treatment as of a piece with the educational enterprise in general. Thus in Chapter 6 it turns out that Reality Therapy is congenial to and readily applicable by classroom teachers in conjunction with their regular pedagogical activities (rather than contradictory to them); and it is also ap-parent that here is an approach to "child rearing" and "mental hygiene" which is *for* parents rather than against them. In a recent issue of *The Saturday Evening Post,* a housewife and mother com-plains bitterly (but justifiably) that psychiatrists have produced a "generation of parent-hating children." It could hardly have been otherwise, for the basic premise of psychoanalytic theory is that neurosis arises from too much training of children by their parents (and other teachers), so that this condition is patently the latter's "fault." Far from helping children to become more mature and accountable, this philosophy has steered young people toward ever deeper delinquency, defiance, and rejection of parents and author-ity.

Thus Reality Therapy is not something which should be the exclusive preoccupation or "property" of a few highly trained (and expensive) specialists. It is the appropriate, indeed the necessary, concern of *everyone,* for its precepts and principles are the foundation of successful, satisfying social life everywhere. Although Freudian psychoanalysts have been arch-critics of our mores, morals, and values, it is doubtful that they could themselves design and direct a viable society, for the very conventions and moral standards which analysts so freely criticize are precisely what keep groups and persons from "falling apart." As Professor C. Wright Mills (the sociologist) and Dr. Richard R. Parlour (a forensic psychiatrist) have recently pointed out, ethical neutrality and anomia cannot provide the *structure* of organization and power and the context of personal identity and meaning which are as essential to individuals as they are to groups. The work of the psychologist, Dr. Perry London, and of anthropologist Jules Henry adds further weight to this opinion.

Now we come to the second of the three R's, *responsibility.* What is it? Glasser says:

> Responsibility, a concept basic to Reality Therapy, is defined as the ability to fulfill one's needs, and to do so in *a way that does not deprive others of the ability to fulfill their needs.* . . . A responsible person also does that which gives him a feeling of self-worth and a feeling that he is worthwhile to others. He is motivated to strive and perhaps endure privation to attain self-worth. When a responsible man says that he will perform a job for us, he will try to accomplish what was asked, both for us and so that he may gain a measure of self-worth for himself. An irresponsible person may or may not do what he says, depending upon how he feels, the effort he has to make, and what is in it for him. He gains neither our respect nor his own, and in time he will suffer or cause others to suffer.

In a recent article, Dr. Glasser has expressed the same general point of view by saying: "People do not act irresponsibly because they are 'ill'; they are 'ill' because they act irresponsibly." This is an emphasis which has been almost totally absent in classical psychoanalysis. For Freud and his many followers, the neurotic's problem is not irresponsibility but lack of "insight." However, many clinicians have discovered that years of analytic questing for this objective often results in less concrete change in a patient's life than a few weeks of work on the problem of personal responsibility, consistency, accountability. (This is confirmed in the writings of Dr. Steve Pratt on the concept of *social contract* and its relation to what Professor Leonard Cottrell has termed "interpersonal competence.") In other words, it's not "insight," "understanding," and "freedom" that the neurotic needs but *commitment*. In the words of an old hymn, our petition can appropriately be:

> Holy Spirit, Right Divine, Truth within my conscience reign,
> Be my King that I may be, firmly bound, forever free.

In keeping with this way of thinking about responsibility, what is to be said about honesty, truthfulness, and integrity? As long as one assumes that the neurotic is typically over-trained in moral matters and that his condition is not in any way dependent upon decisions he himself has made and actions he has taken but is rather an expression of things that have been *done to* him, then the very possibility that dishonesty enters into the picture in any very significant way is excluded, both logically and practically. But when the so-called "sick" person is himself seen as accountable for much of his malaise, dishonesty begins to figure much more prominently. In this book there is not a great deal of explicit emphasis on getting persons who are undergoing therapy to speak the truth; but the therapist himself sets an example of personal openness and integrity, and it is hard to imagine that anyone can learn to be either responsible or realistic without also being truthful. In fact, anyone who makes a practice of misinforming others (and thus being irresponsible), eventually begins to lie to himself, in the sense of rationalizing and excusing his own deviant behavior; and when this happens, he begins to be unrealistic, to "lose contact" with reality.

In light of the widespread and growing interest today in *group* therapy, it may appear to some readers of this book that Dr. Glasser is still too much wedded to individual treatment. Such an impression is misleading. Most of the work at the Ventura School for Girls which is here described involves group methods, as does the work of Dr. G. L. Harrington at the Los Angeles Veterans' Administration Hospital and that of Dr. Willard A. Mainord at the Western State Hospital, in Washington, which are also prominently featured in this book. One of the great advantages of the group approach is that it encourages the development of rectitude, responsibility, and realism so much more rapidly than do the conventional forms of individual treatment.

Now what *is* realism, reality? Although this concept is crucial to Dr. Glasser's approach, in some ways it is the most difficult of all to pin down specifically. Two statements which bear directly on this problem follow:

> In their unsuccessful effort to fulfill their needs, no matter what behavior they choose, all patients have a common characteristic: *They all deny the reality of the world around them.* Some break the law, denying the rules of society; some claim their neighbors are plotting against them, denying the improbability of such behavior. Some are afraid of crowded places, close quarters, airplanes, or elevators, yet they freely admit the irrationality of their fears. Millions drink to blot out the inadequacy they feel but that need not exist if they could learn to be different; and far too many people choose suicide rather than face the reality that they could solve their problems by more responsible behavior. Whether it is a partial denial or the total blotting out of all reality of the chronic back-ward patient in the state hospital, the denial of some or all of reality is common to all patients. Therapy will be successful when they are able to give up denying the world and to recognize that reality not only exists but that they must fulfill their needs within its framework.
>
> . . . The therapist who accepts excuses, ignores reality, or allows the patient to blame his present unhappiness on a parent or on an emotional disturbance can usually make his patient feel good temporarily at the price of evading responsibility. He is only giving the patient "psychiatric kicks," which are no different from the brief kicks he may have obtained from alcohol, pills, or sympathetic friends before consulting the psychiatrist. When they fade, as they soon must, the patient with good reason becomes disillusioned with psychiatry.

Although implied by and embedded in Reality Therapy as a whole, there is a way of thinking about the question of what is and what is not "realistic" which can and perhaps should be made more explicit. From one point of view, it can be argued that all experience is reality of a kind. Phenomenologically, there is certainly nothing *un*real about illicit or perverse sexual behavior, criminal activities, or the total life style of persons we call neurotic or even psychotic. Literally everything that happens is reality. Therefore, some special principle or dimension is needed to make the distinction between reality and irreality fully meaningful. In short-run perspective, there is something "realistic" and "good"— in the sense of pleasurable—about all perverse, criminal, or defensive behavior. Otherwise it simply would not occur. But more precisely speaking, action can be called realistic or unrealistic only when its *remote* as well as immediate consequences are taken into consideration and compared, weighed. If the evil, pain, suffering which ultimately occur as a result of a given action exceed the immediate satisfaction which it produced, that action may be termed unrealistic; whereas, if the satisfaction which ultimately occurs as a result of an action is greater than the immediate effort or sacrifice associated with it, such an action can be called realistic. In the final analysis, it is the capacity to choose wisely between these two types of behavior that we call *reason;* and it is, I think, what the Chicago columnist, Sidney Harris, had in mind when he once characterized the truly educated man as one who knows and can properly appraise the *consequences* of his actions. It is what Alfred Korzybski meant when he spoke of the human capacity for *time-binding;* and it is what I have previously denoted by the expression, *temporal integration.* It is also, I believe, what Dr. Glasser implies when he says, in one of the passages already quoted: "A responsible person . . . is motivated to *strive* and perhaps *endure privation.* . . . An irresponsible person . . . gains neither our respect nor his own, and *in time* he will suffer or cause others to suffer" (italics added).

In a paper entitled "Formations Regarding the Two Principles of Mental Functioning" which appeared in 1911, Freud made a clear distinction between what he called the pleasure principle and the reality principle; and again the distinguishing criterion was a temporal one. However, while praising the reality principle, Freud propounded a therapeutic technique which, paradoxically, glorifies pleasure and permissiveness. It was not that Freud recommended that we totally surrender to the sway of pleasure and live entirely in the present. Rather, his argument was that "conventional morality" is unrealistic in the sense of making more de-

mands for restraint and "repression" than are actually necessary.
Thus he pleaded for what he termed an "intermediate course." He
said:

> We [analysts] are not reformers . . .; we are merely observers;
> but we cannot avoid observing with critical eyes, and we have
> found it impossible to give our support to conventional morality
> [which] demands more sacrifices than it is worth. We do not
> absolve our patients from listening to these criticisms . . . and if
> after they have become independent by the effects of the treat-
> ment they choose some intermediate course . . ., our conscience
> is not burdened whatever the outcome.

Thus the crucial question is: Was Freud's conception of neurosis correct or incorrect? For a generation we have assumed that
his diagnosis of the problem was essentially sound. Today we are
not particularly pleased with the results of treatment predicated on
this view; and Dr. Glasser has given us what I believe is the best
description to date of a radically different approach. Here the
assumption, as we have already seen, is that all "clinical types"
represent *under*-socialization and that therapy, to be consistent and
effective, must in all cases be directed toward getting the individual
to be *more* responsible, *more* realistic, in the sense of being willing
to make immediate sacrifices for long-term (one may almost say
lifelong) satisfactions and gains. Some persons do not live long
enough to reap the full harvest of their virtue—and this we all
recognize as a form of *tragedy*. But the reverse situation is *folly*.
The trouble with "Eat, drink, and be merry, for tomorrow we die"
is that we usually *don't* die tomorrow but instead live on to reap
only too fully the negative consequences of shortsighted pleasure
seeking. The habitual drunkard does not have to be very old to
have lived too long, and it is no accident that he so often either
attempts or successfully commits suicide.

Thus the therapeutic problem, basically, is that of getting another person to abandon what may be called the *primitive* pleasure
principle and to adopt that long-term, enlightened, *wise* pursuit of
pleasure, satisfaction, joy, happiness which the reality principle
implies. An immediate, assured source of pleasure is never will-
ingly given up for a larger but uncertain remote satisfaction. And

an essential aspect of therapy, as of all education, all socialization is that of providing the immature person with some compensation, some substitute satisfaction for the one he is being asked, in his own long-term best interests, to give up. In the ordinary socialization of children, parental love serves this function. In his description of Reality Therapy, Dr. Glasser calls it *involvement,* of which he says:

> Usually the most difficult phase of therapy is the first, the gaining of the involvement that the patient so desperately needs but which he has been unsuccessful in attaining or maintaining up to the time he comes for treatment. Unless the requisite involvement exists between the necessarily responsible therapist and the irresponsible patient, there can be no therapy. The guiding principles of Reality Therapy are directed toward achieving the proper involvement, a completely honest, human relationship in which the patient, for perhaps the first time in his life, realizes that someone cares enough about him not only to accept him but to help him fulfill his needs in the real world.
>
>   . . . How does the therapist become involved with a patient so that the patient can begin to fulfill his needs? The therapist has a difficult task, for he must quickly build a firm emotional relationship with a patient who has failed to establish such relationships in the past. He is aided by recognizing that the patient is desperate for involvement and is suffering because he is not able to fulfill his needs. The patient is looking for a person with whom he can become emotionally involved, someone he can care about and who he can be convinced cares about him, someone who can convince the patient that he will stay with him until he can better fulfill his needs.

For some readers, the foregoing discussion of involvement will be reminiscent of the psychoanalytic concept of transference, but there are marked differences, both in regard to method and objective. Psychoanalytic transference is said to be best achieved when the therapist remains inexplicit and shadowy as a person, onto whom the patient can "project" his neurotic, harsh, unrealistic, anxiety-arousing expectations of all authoritative "father figures." The therapist then, at strategic points, "reveals" himself as really kind, accepting, permissive, and in this way supposedly brings about the needed modification, or "softening," of the superego. By contrast, the objective of Reality Therapy is to support and strengthen, never to weaken, the functioning of conscience; and the method of choice involves honesty, concern, personal authenticity, and confrontation of the kind Dr. Glasser describes.

But is there not an ultimate and fatal paradox here? How can one hold that a neurotic or otherwise "delinquent" person is "responsible" and at the same time take the position that such a person needs or can benefit from treatment? Does not the very concept of treatment, or help, imply a certain helplessness and *lack* of responsibility on the part of the person who is "in trouble"? Language can at this point play an insidious trick on us if we are not extremely careful. The difficulty in the case of the irresponsible (neurotic, delinquent) person is precisely that he is *not* acting responsibly; and his great need is that of learning to behave *more* responsibly and thus *better* fulfill his own long-term needs—as well as those of society as a whole. In the present volume, Dr. Glasser is not saying that patients are *responsible for* what has happened in the past; instead, he is saying that they have not been, and are not now, *living responsibly*. There's a great difference between these two statements. And therapeutic (educative) influence from whatever quarter ought to be in the direction of helping patients improve their capacity and desire to live more responsibly, prudently, wisely from now on. Thus the concept of responsibility, far from implying or stressing the evil in man is rather one which sees and builds upon his potentialities *for good*; and it is therefore decidedly optimistic and hopeful rather than cynical or pessimistic.

Enough has now been said to show that Reality Therapy is "different." Now we must ask: Is it also *better*? Clinical evidence from several sources is cited in this book which strongly suggests an affirmative answer. No one, at this point, is claiming that the evidence is definitive. But as a research psychologist I can attest that there is today much additional supporting data of a thoroughly empirical nature and that the premises of Reality Therapy are rapidly gaining credence in many quarters. Its promise for the future therefore seems to be very bright, and the present volume fills a real need for a simply written and yet clinically informed and sophisticated description of this approach and its working assumptions. The reader will enjoy the author's clear, lively style of writing and will profit from an account which, I predict, is destined to arouse much popular as well as scientific interest.

O. Hobart Mowrer, Ph.D.
Research Professor of Psychology
University of Illinois

Acknowledgments

Toward the end of my psychiatric training I found myself in the uncomfortable position of doubting much that I had been taught. My teachers implied that there was a great deal more to be learned in the field, but only a very few questioned the basic tenets of conventional psychiatry. One of these few was my last teacher, Dr. G. L. Harrington. When I hesitatingly expressed my own concern, he reached across the desk, shook my hand and said "join the club." For the past eight years as I progressed from student to colleague he has continued to work with me to develop the concepts of Reality Therapy. Nothing that I can say briefly or in many pages could express how grateful I am for the time he generously spent to make this possible.

Concepts, however, do not make a book. They must be clarified and tested by objective critics, preferably with no ax to grind except that of logic and consistency. My cousin, Robert Lloyd Glasser, an aeronautical engineer by profession and a psychiatric critic by avocation, spent hundreds of hours critically editing the manuscript and when he finished Harold Grove, my editor at Harper's, stepped in. Their combined efforts have made the book immeasurably more clear and consistent.

I would also like to thank Mrs. Beatrice Dolan, the superintendent of the Ventura School, and her staff and Dr. Thomas Gucker, of the Los Angeles Orthopaedic Hospital and his staff for their continued warm support in helping me put these concepts into practice. And finally my appreciation to my wife and family for their help, encouragement, and tolerance.

Note to the Paperback Edition

Much has happened since Reality Therapy was published in 1965. The ideas that seemed so radical then have been widely accepted and put into practice all over the United States and Canada. Nevertheless, you may have some difficulty finding a Reality Therapist, because the ideas are used more in schools, correctional services, mental hospitals, and halfway houses than by private practitioners. This is because public institutions are desperate for ideas their staff can use successfully, and when they put these ideas into practice they find they work. It is from these successes that the word has spread. Private practitioners dealing with smaller case loads and accountable to no one except themselves feel less urgency and tend to be traditional in both training and practice. Therefore, even though Reality Therapy may make sense to you, as yet it is not easy to find a Reality Therapist.

To help change this situation we have established the Institute for Reality Therapy in Los Angeles, where we give intensive training in the use of these ideas to anyone who works with people. We are more interested in need than we are in formal credentials, because we recognize that most of the gut-level mental health work in this country is done by people without extensive training, such as parents, probation officers, teachers, school administrators, ministers, drug rehabilitation counselors, and psychiatric technicians, to cite some of the people who have studied with us. Nevertheless, we maintain such a high standard in our seminars that many of the highly trained professionals who make up about half of those who attend tell me how much they benefit from studying with others who have less-formal credentials. Certainly one of the flaws in my psychiatric residency was the way we were trained separately, away from the nurses, aides, social workers, and psychologists who worked with us.

Until we succeed in reaching more people, especially people in private practice, I suggest that if you want Reality Therapy and find there is no one near you that we have trained, read this book carefully and then ask around. It is your life; don't be afraid to ask pointed questions from someone to whom you are prepared to bare your soul. Ask social workers, psychologists, and marriage and family counselors; they are more likely to use new ideas than psychiatrists. If you find one who is familiar with these ideas and who uses them in his work, talk with him a few times and see if you seem to be on the right track. The important thing to look for is someone who not only understands Reality Therapy but who also is warm and friendly, someone you feel comfortable with, someone who is not distant, objective, or aloof. A good Reality Therapist is your friend; he talks to you honestly and treats you as a human being who has problems that can be solved now, through more responsible behavior. It is next to impossible to get help from someone with whom you are not comfortable.

Finally, many people have written to me telling me how they have used these ideas to help themselves. In a later book, *The Identity Society,* I describe this self-help approach more fully, but the basic concepts are all here. Read Chapter 1 ten times and you will find there is more there than you first realized. Discussing Reality Therapy with a friend can also be very helpful.

We must all realize that while we may be a product of our history, we cannot change what has happened to us. We must accept the fact that it is not profitable to sit around year after year and cry about our misfortunes and, at the same time, excuse our inability to help ourselves on the basis of that same misfortune. All we can change is what we are doing now, and if we can become more responsible most of our trouble will clear. If this seems hopeful, I mean it to be so; most of us are not doomed by circumstances to suffer. Although it is hard for us to admit, we choose our misery and we make it our way of life. We do so out of weakness, but through Reality Therapy we can gain the strength to make better choices and in most instances to lead a much more satisfying life. I appreciate your interest in my work, and for further information about what we do, write:

WILLIAM GLASSER, M.D., President
Institute for Reality Therapy
11633 San Vicente Boulevard
Los Angeles, California 90049

Part I | THEORY

Introduction

Reality Therapy is an effective psychiatric treatment different from that generally accepted today. Based on psychiatric theory which also differs greatly from conventional or traditional psychiatry, it is applicable to all people with psychiatric problems. This book will describe Reality Therapy, explain in detail how it differs from conventional psychiatry, and show its successful application to the treatment of juvenile delinquents, chronic mental hospital patients, private psychiatric patients, and disturbed children in the school classroom.

The first part of the book explains the basic concepts of Reality Therapy, a treatment applicable to both groups and individuals with psychiatric problems. Before we can understand treatment, however, we must have some idea of what it is that psychiatrists treat—what is wrong with the many people who seek psychiatric help. After the essential problem of all those who need psychiatric treatment is made clear, the development of Reality Therapy as a logical method of treatment is presented.

1 | The Basic Concepts of Reality Therapy

WHAT IS WRONG WITH THOSE WHO
NEED PSYCHIATRIC TREATMENT?

What is it that psychiatrists attempt to treat? What is wrong with the man in a mental hospital who claims he is Jesus, with the boy in and out of reform schools who has stolen thirty-eight cars, the woman who has continual crippling migraine headaches, the child who refuses to learn in school and disrupts the class with temper outbursts, the man who must lose a promotion because he is afraid to fly, and the bus driver who suddenly goes berserk and drives his bus load of people fifty miles from its destination in a careening danger-filled ride?

Do these widely different behaviors indicate different psychiatric problems requiring a variety of explanations, or are they manifestations of one underlying difficulty? We believe that, regardless of how he expresses his problem, everyone who needs psychiatric treatment suffers from one basic inadequacy: he is unable to fulfill his essential needs. The severity of the symptom reflects the degree to which the individual is unable to fulfill his needs. No one can explain exactly why one person expresses his problem with a stomach ulcer while another fears to enter an elevator; but whatever the symptom, it disappears when the person's needs are successfully fulfilled.

Further, we must understand that not only is the psychiatric

5

problem a manifestation of a person's inability to fulfill his needs, but no matter how irrational or inadequate his behavior may seem to us, it has meaning and validity to him. The best he can do in an uncomfortable, often miserable condition, his behavior is his attempt to solve his particular variety of the basic problem of all psychiatric patients, the inability to fulfill his needs.

In their unsuccessful effort to fulfill their needs, no matter what behavior they choose, all patients have a common characteristic: *they all deny the reality of the world around them.* Some break the law, denying the rules of society; some claim their neighbors are plotting against them, denying the improbability of such behavior. Some are afraid of crowded places, close quarters, airplanes, or elevators, yet they freely admit the irrationality of their fears. Millions drink to blot out the inadequacy they feel but that need not exist if they could learn to be different; and far too many people choose suicide rather than face the reality that they could solve their problems by more responsible behavior. Whether it is a partial denial or the total blotting out of all reality of the chronic backward patient in the state hospital, the denial of some or all of reality is common to all patients. Therapy will be successful when they are able to give up denying the world and recognize that reality not only exists but that they must fulfill their needs within its framework.

A therapy that leads all patients toward reality, toward grappling successfully with the tangible and intangible aspects of the real world, might accurately be called a therapy toward reality, or simply *Reality Therapy.*

As mentioned above, it is not enough to help a patient face reality; he must also learn to fulfill his needs. Previously when he attempted to fulfill his needs in the real world, he was unsuccessful. He began to deny the real world and to try to fulfill his needs as if some aspects of the world did not exist or in defiance of their existence. A psychotic patient who lives in a world of his own and a delinquent boy who repeatedly breaks the law are common examples of these two conditions. Even a man with a stomach ulcer who seems to be facing reality in every way is upon investigation often found to be attempting more than he can cope with, and his ulcer is his body's reaction to the excess stress. Therefore, to do

Reality Therapy the therapist must not only be able to help the patient accept the real world, but he must then further help him fulfill his needs in the real world so that he will have no inclination in the future to deny its existence.

HOW DO WE FULFILL OUR NEEDS?

Before discussing the basic needs themselves, we must clarify the process through which they are fulfilled. Briefly, *we must be involved with other people,* one at the very minimum, but hopefully many more than one. At all times in our lives we must have at least one person who cares about us and whom we care for ourselves. If we do not have this essential person, we will not be able to fulfill our basic needs. Although the person usually is in some direct relationship with us as a mother is to a child or a teacher is to a pupil, he need not be that close as long as we have a strong feeling of his existence and he, no matter how distant, has an equally strong feeling of our existence. One characteristic is essential in the other person: he must be in touch with reality himself and able to fulfill his own needs within the world. A man marooned on a desert isle or confined in a solitary cell may be able to fulfill his needs enough to survive if he knows that someone he cares for cares about him and his condition. If the prisoner or castaway loses the conviction that this essential human cares about what is happening to him, he will begin to lose touch with reality, his needs will be more and more unfulfilled, and he may die or become insane.

A graphic example in which two people sustained each other through severe hardship followed a recent airplane crash in the snowy wilds of northern Canada. A young woman and an experienced pilot lived forty-nine days without food before they were rescued. Not only were they in remarkably good physical condition but they did not even describe their total experience as horrible. Both said that they sustained each other and had faith in ultimate rescue. Although they were involved with each other through the circumstances, both were also involved enough with others so that they did not give up. They survived by not losing touch with reality and fulfilling their needs as well as they could.

Without the key person through whom we gain the strength and encouragement to cope with reality, we try desperately in many unrealistic ways to fulfill our needs. In doing so our efforts range throughout the whole gamut of psychiatric problems from mild anxiety to complete denial of reality. Therefore, essential to fulfillment of our needs is a person, perferably a group of people, with whom we are emotionally involved *from the time we are born to the time we die.* Much of what we call senility or senile psychosis is nothing more than the reaction of aged people to isolation. They may be physically near many people but no one is any longer involved with them. A beautifully written example is the play *The Silver Whistle* in which a young ne'er-do-well disguises himself as an old man in order to get into what he thinks is the warmth and comfort of an old folks' home. Here he finds the occupants unnecessarily decrepit and senile. By helping them to become involved with each other he restores them to functioning much better than they had dreamed possible. Having had a similar experience working with a ninety-five-year-old patient, I can testify to the almost miraculous effect of getting a very old man involved in life again after he had thought it impossible. From a weak, bedridden, senile man he became a vigorous, self-sufficient, active member of the sanitarium patient group, all in a period of a little over three months.

Unless a patient becomes actively involved with at least one person in a better way than he is now involved with anyone, he will be unable to fulfill his needs. Well-meaning advice always fails—patients can't straighten up and fly right when someone points out reality to them when there is not sufficient involvement. Without it no one can be helped to help himself fulfill his needs.

THE BASIC NEEDS

Now that we have seen that an involvement with someone you care for and who you are convinced cares for you is the key to fulfilling the basic needs, we can proceed to a discussion of the needs themselves. For therapy we recognize two basic needs— needs which cause suffering unless they are fulfilled.

It is generally accepted that all humans have the same physiological and psychological needs. Competent people may describe or label these needs differently, but no one seriously disputes that in all cultures and in all degrees of civilization men have the same essential needs. It is also generally accepted that needs do not vary with age, sex, or race. A Chinese infant girl has the same needs as a Swedish king. The fulfillment of the physiological needs for food, warmth, and rest are rarely the concern of psychiatry. Psychiatry must be concerned with two basic psychological needs: *the need to love and be loved and the need to feel that we are worthwhile to ourselves and to others.* Helping patients fulfill these two needs is the basis of Reality Therapy.

Although men of all societies, classes, colors, creeds, and intellectual capacity have the same needs, they vary remarkably in their ability to fulfill them. In every area of the world, including the most economically and culturally advanced, there are many people whose psychological needs are not satisfied, who are unable to give and receive love and who have no feeling of worth either to themselves or to others. These people are the concern of psychiatry, either because they directly present themselves for help, or because their behavior leads their family or the community to compel them to seek out-patient help or be placed in a psychiatric or correctional institution.

The proper role of psychiatry will always be to help people help themselves to fulfill their needs, given a reasonable opportunity to do so. Thus, a person with family and friends who care about him and with the opportunity to work in a reasonable job, who cannot fulfill his needs is considered to have a psychiatric problem. If, however, no one cares about him and he can obtain no gainful work, the problem may be more environmental than psychiatric. For example, if a Negro student at a newly integrated southern college is unable to study effectively, he is not necessarily suffering from psychological problems. If a potentially capable white student from a loving family flunks out of the same college, however, psychological guidance is more likely needed.

To develop the underlying problem—*we all have the same needs but we vary in our ability to fulfill them*—we must examine the generally accepted psychological needs in more detail.

First is the need to love and be loved. In all its forms, ranging from friendship through mother love, family love, and conjugal love, this need drives us to continuous activity in search of satisfaction. From birth to old age we need to love and be loved. Throughout our lives, our health and our happiness will depend upon our ability to do so. To either love or to allow ourselves to be loved is not enough; we must do both. When we cannot satisfy our total need for love, we will without fail suffer and react with many familiar psychological symptoms, from mild discomfort through anxiety and depression to complete withdrawal from the world around us.

Equal in importance to the need for love is the need to feel that we are worthwhile both to ourselves and to others. Although the two needs are separate, a person who loves and is loved will usually feel that he is a worthwhile person, and one who is worthwhile is usually someone who is loved and who can give love in return. While this is usually the case, it is not always so. For example, although an overindulged child may receive an abundance of love, the parents do not make the critical distinction between loving him and accepting his behavior, good or bad. Certainly the child should be loved, but love need not mean a blanket approval of everything he does. The child knows the difference between right and wrong behavior and is frustrated because receiving love for behavior that he knows is wrong does not allow him to feel worthwhile. In this situation, he reacts in all the familiar spoiled-child patterns in an effort to get his parents to enforce some behavioral limits and some achievement standards along with their love. When the parents do so, the child's behavior improves. A beautiful and capable woman often finds herself in a similarly uncomfortable position when she is recognized only for her beauty. Therefore, an important part of fulfilling our need to be worthwhile depends upon the ability to see that being the object of someone's love does not in itself give us worth.

But, whether we are loved or not, *to be worthwhile we must maintain a satisfactory standard of behavior.* To do so we must learn to correct ourselves when we do wrong and to credit ourselves when we do right. If we do not evaluate our own behavior, or having evaluated it, we do not act to improve our conduct where it is below our standards, we will not fulfill our need to be worthwhile and we will suffer as acutely as when we fail to love or be loved. Morals, standards, values, or right and wrong behavior are all intimately related to the fulfillment of our need for self-worth and, as will be explained later, a necessary part of Reality Therapy.

Thus, when we are unable to fulfill one or both of our needs, we feel pain or discomfort in some form. The pain, which may show itself throughout the whole central nervous system from a simple spinal reflex to our highest centers of abstract thought, motivates us to some activity to try to relieve it. If we sit on a hot radiator, we leap up to avoid burning ourselves. Similarly, but not as dramatically, if we are unable to love, we may shun people to avoid the pain of being in contact with those we cannot admit to ourselves that we need because we are afraid of rejection. Trying to tell ourselves that we do not need other people, we are like the fox who momentarily feels less pain when she walks away muttering, "Sour grapes." Aesop did not reveal whether or not the fox consulted a psychiatrist for her denial of reality, but when a sour-grapes person who is unable to love removes himself from society, few would deny that he has a psychiatric problem. The problem is caused by his inability to behave so that he can give and receive love. He must become motivated to change his behavior because as long as he shuns people, he will continue to suffer. The only means by which we feel he can become motivated to change is to look honestly at his own behavior to determine whether or not it contributes to fulfilling his needs. Unless he can give up the sour-grapes attitude, face reality, and admit to himself that the grapes are probably sweet and that he must try harder to reach them, he will never fulfill his needs.

Learning to fulfill our needs must begin early in infancy and continue all our lives. If we fail to learn we will suffer, and this suffering always drives us to try unrealistic means to fulfill our needs. A person who does not learn as a little child to give and receive love may spend the rest of his life unsuccessfully trying to love. A woman, for example, may become involved in series of unhappy romances in which she uses sex in an unrealistic attempt to gain and give love. Only when she learns that there are better ways to attain love will she give up her unhappy, unsatisfactory behavior. A related example is a happily married woman whose husband dies. If she cannot adjust to her loss realistically and fulfill her need for love, she may follow the course of the woman in the previous example.

From the discussion we can draw an important conclusion. If we do not learn to fulfill our needs, we will suffer all of our lives; the younger and the more thoroughly we learn, the more satisfactory our lives will be. However, even if we learn at a young age to fulfill our needs moderately well, we may not be able to continue to do so all of our lives. From time to time in everyone's life the world and our situation in it changes, requiring us to learn and relearn to fulfill our needs under different conditions and stresses. Whether we learn to fulfill our needs when we are young or at any time later, we must stay involved with people. Perhaps at first it is mother and father, then friends, teachers, lover, husband or wife, children, and grandchildren, but there must always be someone with whom we feel intimately involved. If at any time in our lives the involvement is broken, we will very quickly become unable to satisfy our needs. We might say, therefore, that all people who have any kind of serious psychiatric problem *are at that time* lacking the proper involvement with someone—and, lacking that involvement, are unable to satisfy their needs.

We know, therefore, that *at the time any person comes for psychiatric help he is lacking the most critical factor for fulfilling his needs, a person whom he genuinely cares about and who he feels genuinely cares about him.* Sometimes it is obvious that the patient has no close relationships. Many times, however, especially in patients who are functioning fairly well and come to a psychiatrist in private practice, the lack of involvement is not apparent. Patients may have devoted wives, friends, and family, but they still are unable to fulfill their needs. Despite the presence of people who claim they care, the patient is either not able to accept their love, or he does not care for them. What appear to be satisfactory relationships are not satisfactory for him, a condition often graphically illustrated by the case of many suicides. A person who commits suicide may have many people who care about him and he may be successful in his work, yet still leave a note describing the overwhelming loneliness and isolation he feels. Therefore, to obtain help in therapy the patient must gain or regain involvement, first with the therapist and then with others. His problem and the accompanying symptoms will disappear once he is able to become involved and fulfill his needs.

Fulfilling his needs, however, is a part of his present life; it has nothing to do with his past no matter how miserable his previous life has been. It is not only possible, it is desirable to ignore his past and work in the present because, contrary to almost universal belief, nothing which happened in his past, no matter how it may have affected him then or now, will make any difference once he learns to fulfill his needs at the present time.

Having established that we are concerned with involvement and what the patient is doing now in contrast to the usual emphasis on his past life, we must also state that we do not concern ourselves with unconscious mental processes. We do not deny that they exist as demonstrated vividly by our dreams, but they are unnecessary to the essential process of helping a patient fulfill his needs, a process which we have found must be completely conscious to be effective. The difference between Reality Therapy and conventional psychiatry on these and other important issues is discussed in detail in the next chapter of this book.

RESPONSIBILITY

Responsibility, a concept basic to Reality Therapy, is here defined as the ability to fulfill one's needs, and to do so *in a way that does not deprive others of the ability to fulfill their needs*. To illustrate, a responsible person can give and receive love. If a girl, for example, falls in love with a responsible man, we would expect him either to return her love or to let her know in a considerate way that he appreciates her affection but that he does not share her feelings. If he takes advantage of her love to gain some material or sexual end, we would not consider him responsible.

A responsible person also does that which gives him a feeling of self-worth and a feeling that he is worthwhile to others. He is motivated to strive and perhaps endure privation to attain self-worth. When a responsible man says that he will perform a job for us, he will try to accomplish what was asked, both for us and so that he may gain a measure of self-worth for himself. An irresponsible person may or may not do what he says depending upon how he feels, the effort he has to make, and what is in it for him. He gains neither our respect nor his own, and in time he will suffer or cause others to suffer.

Acquiring responsibility is a complicated, lifelong problem. *Although we are given unchanging needs from birth to death, needs which, if left unsatisfied, cause us or others to suffer, we are not naturally endowed with the ability to fulfill them.* If the ability to fulfill our needs were as much a part of man as are the needs themselves, there would be no psychiatric problems. This ability must, however, be learned. Five hundred thousand people in our mental hospitals alone testify that it is not an easy task; but, difficult as responsibility is to learn, I do not wish to imply that the majority of our population are irresponsible or unsuccessful in learning to fulfill their needs. Behaving responsibly themselves, most people strive to create an environment in which both by example and direct teaching they communicate this knowledge to those they love. We are not, however, directly concerned with those who have learned to lead responsible lives. *Our concern is with those who have not learned, or who have lost the ability— those who fill our mental hospitals and prisons, our psychiatric clinics and offices.*

Throughout the remainder of this book, *these people are described as irresponsible.* Their behavior is their effort, inadequate and unrealistic as it may be, to fulfill their needs.

Two groups of people who must be classed as irresponsible by our definition are generally not our concern as psychotherapists. First are those who may fulfill their needs at the price of preventing others from doing so. In a totalitarian society like Nazi Germany, Hitler might have been considered highly responsible by those who believed in his perverse ideas. Through his behavior he gained love and respect from those who felt as he did, but he made the rules. Those who value a free society could not accept his rules and still give and receive love or feel self-worth. In Nazi Germany, a responsible man, by our definition, would have been placed in a concentration camp, and many were. In a free society a Nazi is always irresponsible. His behavior is not socially acceptable and would not fulfill his needs.

There are many others in this first group who are irresponsible only in part—much of their behavior is responsible and does lead to need fulfillment. Among them we find some prominent political leaders in the South who believe that the Negro is inferior and dange-ous to white society. To the extent that these men behave in a way that causes others to suffer they are irresponsible.

The second group consists of those who only partially fulfill their needs but are not the concern of psychotherapists because they do not harm others and do not ask for help themselves. Among these people may be homosexuals who lead meaningful, productive lives, recluses, and various eccentrics.

In consonance with our emphasis on responsibility and irresponsibility, we who practice Reality Therapy advocate dispensing with the common psychiatric labels, such as neurosis and psychosis, which tend to categorize and stereotype people. Limiting our descriptions to the behavior which the patient manifests, we would, for example, describe a man who believes that he is President Johnson as irresponsible, followed by a brief description of his unrealistic behavior and thinking. Calling him psychotic or schizophrenic immediately places him in a mental illness category which separates him from most of us, the label thereby serving to compound his problem. Through our description it can immediately be understood that he is unsuccessful in fulfilling his needs. He has given up trying to do so as John Jones and is now trying as President Johnson, a logical delusion for a man who feels isolated and inadequate. The description *irresponsible* is much more precise, indicating that our job is to help him to become more responsible so that he will be able to satisfy his needs as himself. It is evident, however, that *neurotic, psychotic, schizophrenic,* and other similar terms are a part of our language, both popular and scientific. Because dispensing with them suddenly would be artificial and misleading to many readers, they are used occasionally in the remainder of this book. We suggest, however, that these labels be considered only as descriptions of irresponsibility, nothing more. We hope that the reader will try to substitute *responsible* for *mental health* and *irresponsible* for *mental illness* and its many subcategories. Accepting this change in terminology will in itself help us approach those we treat not as mentally ill, but as people who need to become involved with us to fulfill their needs and thereby improve the behavior which brings them to our attention.

THE TEACHING OF RESPONSIBILITY

The teaching of responsibility is the most important task of all higher animals, man most certainly included. Except for man this task is performed primarily under the pressure of instinct—instinct related directly to the continuation of the species. Animals have only a few months to learn to survive; if the time is not spent in intensive training, they do not live. The coyote is a wonderful example of a species that has persisted despite unfavorable conditions. Even the ingenuity of man has not succeeded in destroying the coyote because it is wary and wise. The coyote mother impresses her pups almost from birth with the need to take care of themselves, to depend on their physical and mental capacities, and above all, to be aware of danger. The pups evidently sense the intensity of their teacher and learn their lesson well. They survive considerable odds and continue to live under the most adverse conditions.

As the many instances of abandoned children show, man is not driven by instinct to care for and teach responsibility to his children. In place of instinct, however, man has developed the intellectual capacity to be able to teach responsibility well. Children ordinarily learn by means of a loving relationship with responsible parents, an involvement which implies parental teaching and parental example. In addition, responsibility is taught by responsible relatives, teachers, ministers, and friends with whom they become involved. The responsible parent creates the necessary involvement with his child and teaches him responsibility through the proper combination of love and discipline. Although the means by which every responsible man was exposed to love and discipline may not be apparent, careful investigation will, we feel, always show that it did occur. People who are not at some time in their lives, preferably early, exposed intimately to others who care enough about them both to love and discipline them will not learn to be responsible. For that failure they suffer all their lives.

The words "preferably early" used above are important; they

mean that the younger we are exposed to love and discipline the easier and the better we will learn responsibility. That it can be taught *only* to the young is not true—responsibility can be learned at any age. Nevertheless, it is easier to learn correctly at first than to overcome previous bad learning. Consider the problems in trying to correct a defective golf swing, bad grammar, or poor manners. Learning how to study in college is much harder than learning in primary or even secondary school. Similarly, responsibility should be learned early at home and in school rather than later from a psychiatrist.

Few parents will argue with the statement that many children do not learn responsibility easily. Children do not know that what seems easy to them will not fulfill their needs, so almost from infancy they struggle against the reality that they must learn from their parents how to fulfill their needs. Later, when they are old enough to recognize reality, they test their parents with irresponsible behavior in the same way that psychiatric patients test their therapists. Through discipline tempered with love, parents must teach their children to behave better. The child learns thereby that the parents care.

Children want to become responsible, but they won't accept discipline and learn better ways unless they feel the parents care enough to show them actively the responsible way to behave.

For example, the other night our five-year-old son was asked if he wanted to use the large bathtub, which was full, to splash and play. In his own inimitable way he said no, probably because he recognized that allowing him in the big tub was easier for us than filling his smaller tub. He wanted to assert his independence of our wishes, a very common but trying five-year-old characteristic. Asked again, he repeated his refusal, whereupon his ten-year-old sister flew out of her room, shedding her clothes, and popped into the big tub, a real treat for her. Immediately the five-year-old started to scream that he really wanted to bathe in it himself. I had to pick up fifty pounds of tantrum and place him in his own tub where he continued to wail his protests.

When he realized that his complaints were doing no good he became quiet and I went in to talk to him. I said, "Let me give you some good advice. Do you know what advice is?" He did, so I told him, "Never say no when you mean yes," and I explained this a little more with several examples from previous behavior. Later I heard him telling his grandmother, "Dad gave me some good advice," and repeating what I said with great understanding. He learned the beginning of an important lesson. Too many of us fail to fulfill our needs because we say no rather then yes, or perhaps later in life, yes when we should say no. If I had given in to his tantrum he would have learned nothing. In his attempts to find out if I really cared, he judged me first by what I did, then by what I said, much as all psychiatric patients do with their therapists. Parents must continually act responsibly when dealing with their children in order to maintain the involvement. Those whose actions do not demonstrate responsibility to their children lose involvement and raise irresponsible children who have to test others in the world to try to gain the involvement essential to fulfilling their needs. As juvenile delinquents always do, they often deny reality during the testing, and then they may be in serious trouble.

Another common example is the child who wants to watch television even though he has not done his homework. By promising, begging, threatening, and cajoling his parents, all in an effort to evade his responsibility, he sometimes gets his way, but he has failed to learn about reality. Confronted in school with his homework not completed, the child will often blame his parents and not himself, thus further compounding his irresponsibility. Later when he is faced with a difficult situation, not having learned responsibility, he is unprepared to cope with it. *Parents who are willing to suffer the pain of the child's intense anger by firmly holding him to the responsible course are teaching him a lesson that will help him all his life.* Parents who do not do so are setting the pattern for future irresponsibility which prevents the child from fulfilling the need to feel worthwhile.

The parents must not only hold the child to the correct course of action, they must also show by example that they are capable of taking the responsible course. Parents who have no self-discipline cannot successfully discipline a child. A parent who sits watching television, who never reads a book or demonstrates any of the values of using his intellect, will be hard pressed to teach the value of doing well in school through diligent study. The child who does not learn both by example and instruction will not respect his parents. If they continue to fail him, he may cease to love them because, in a sense, they are depriving him of a chance to fulfill his needs. When discipline is reasonable and understandable, and when the parents' own behavior is consistent with their demands on the child, he will love and respect them even though his surface attitude may not always show it. The parents must understand that the child needs responsible parents and that *taking the responsible course will never permanently alienate the child*. An appreciation of this one simple fact greatly aids parents in teaching their children responsibility.

In essence, we gain self-respect through discipline and closeness to others through love. Discipline must always have within it the element of love. "I care enough about you to force you to act in a better way, in a way you will learn through experience to know, and I already know, is the right way." Similarly, love must always have an element of discipline. "I love you because you are a worthwhile person, because I respect you and feel you respect me as well as yourself."

We are continually intrigued by stories such as *Of Human Bondage,* by Somerset Maugham, in which the hero falls in love with an irresponsible, unloving heroine who has no ability to fulfill her needs. In this story, which reflects many real situations, both hero and heroine were basically irresponsible; the man knew that he was doing wrong, but it took him a long book to stop. Only by becoming more responsible did he extricate himself from a degrading and irresponsible involvement. When he did, he saw clearly what a fool he had been.

The universal appeal of the test of responsibility in the path of temptation has made it a favorite literary theme starting with the story of Adam and Eve. In the passive position of reader we may or may not care whether irresponsibility or responsibility wins— we are intrigued by the contrast. Each time responsibility is challenged the reader tests himself without having to pay the price for failure.

In summary then, we learn responsibility through involvements with responsible fellow human beings, preferably loving parents who will love and discipline us properly, who are intelligent enough to allow us freedom to try out our newly acquired responsibility as soon as we show readiness to do so.

REALITY THERAPY

In the preceding pages we have established the theoretical groundwork for Reality Therapy. We have seen that patients, no matter what their psychiatric complaint, suffer from a universal defect: they are unable to fulfill their needs in a realistic way and have taken some less realistic way in their unsuccessful attempts to do so. Because they are suffering or causing others to suffer, they may either voluntarily see a psychiatrist or be forced to see one. The process by which the psychiatrist guides them so that they can face reality and fulfill their needs is called Reality Therapy.

Although the presentation throughout this book is from a professional standpoint, that is, directed toward psychiatrists, social workers, or psychologists, we must remember that many other people do therapy—at least in the sense of helping people better fulfill their needs. Anyone using the general principles of Reality Therapy who attempts to help a person help himself toward more responsible behavior does nothing basically different from psychiatrists or for that matter different from parents who try to the best of their ability to raise a child to be a responsible citizen. Although teachers, counselors, parole officers, scoutmasters, ministers, athletic coaches, and others who work with people employ what might be called therapeutic principles, it is psychiatrists and social scientists who are given the specific assignment of guiding the most irresponsible people toward more responsibility. Teachers and others are not usually involved with the most irresponsible people, nor are they necessarily working directly toward the specific therapy goal of increasing responsibility. Nevertheless, the major difference between therapy and common guidance that is effective is in intensity, not in kind.

Therapy is a special kind of teaching or training which attempts to accomplish in a relatively short, intense period what should have been established during normal growing up. The more irresponsible the person, the more he has to learn about acceptable realistic behavior in order to fulfill his needs. However, the drug addict, the chronic alcoholic, and the severely psychotic are examples of deeply irresponsible people with whom it is difficult to gain sufficient involvement so that they can learn or relearn better ways to fulfill their needs.

Easy or difficult as its application may be in any particular case, the specialized learning situation which we call Reality Therapy is made up of three separate but intimately interwoven procedures. First, there is the involvement; the therapist must become so involved with the patient that the patient can begin to face reality and see how his behavior is unrealistic. Second, the therapist must reject the behavior which is unrealistic but still accept the patient and maintain his involvement with him. Last, and necessary in varying degrees depending upon the patient, the therapist must teach the patient better ways to fulfill his needs within the confines of reality.

Usually the most difficult phase of therapy is the first, the gaining of the involvement that the patient so desperately needs but which he has been unsuccessful in attaining or maintaining up to the time he comes for treatment. Unless the requisite involvement exists between the necessarily responsible therapist and the irresponsible patient, there can be no therapy. The guiding principles of Reality Therapy are directed toward achieving the proper involvement, a completely honest, human relationship in which the patient, for perhaps the first time in his life, realizes that someone cares enough about him not only to accept him but to help him fulfill his needs in the real world.

THE INVOLVEMENT

How does the therapist become involved with a patient so that the patient can begin to fulfill his needs? The therapist has a difficult task, for he must quickly build a firm emotional relationship with a patient who has failed to establish such relationships in the past. He is aided by recognizing that the patient is desperate for involvement and suffering because he is not able to fulfill his needs. The patient is looking for a person with whom he can become emotionally involved, someone he can care about and who he can be convinced cares about him, someone who can convince the patient that he will stay with him until he can better fulfill his needs. To the therapist struggling with a patient and finding it difficult to become involved, this desperation is often hard to see. Despite his great need for involvement, the patient may resist because he has been disappointed too many times in the past when he tried to find someone with whom to become involved. His resistance is his way of testing the sincerity and responsibility of the therapist. The title psychiatrist means little to a patient: he will test him for the kind of person he is, and if the patient finds him lacking, there will be no involvement.

The ability of the therapist to get involved is the major skill of doing Reality Therapy, but it is most difficult to describe. How does one put into words the building of a strong emotional relationship quickly between two relative strangers? And when the patient does not want to be in therapy—as often occurs with delinquents—or does not even know that he *is* in therapy—as sometimes occurs with severely withdrawn patients in a mental hospital—the task is particularly difficult.

One way to attempt an understanding of how involvement occurs is to describe the qualities necessary to the therapist. The more a person has these qualities, the better able he will be to use the principles of Reality Therapy to develop the proper involvement.

The therapist must be a very responsible person—tough, interested, human, and sensitive. He must be able to fulfill his own needs and must be willing to discuss some of his own struggles so that the patient can see that acting responsibly is possible though sometimes difficult. Neither aloof, superior, nor sacrosanct, he must never imply that what he does, what he stands for, or what he values is unimportant. He must have the strength to become involved, to have his values tested by the patient, and to withstand intense criticism by the person he is trying to help. Every fault and defect may be picked apart by the patient. Willing to admit that, like the patient, he is far from perfect, the therapist must nevertheless show that a person can act responsibly even if it takes great effort.

The therapist must always be strong, never expedient. He must withstand the patient's requests for sympathy, for an excess of sedatives, for justification of his actions no matter how the patient pleads or threatens. Never condoning an irresponsible action on the patient's part, he must be willing to watch the patient suffer if that helps him toward responsibility. Therefore, to practice Reality Therapy takes strength, not only the strength for the therapist to lead a responsible life himself, but also the added strength both to stand up steadily to patients who wish him to accede to their irresponsibility, and to continue to point out reality to them no matter how hard they struggle against it.

Most patients realize that their behavior is deviant, that they are *different*. Even if they do not know it immediately, they are often made aware of it forcibly because society segregates them in mental hospitals, prisons, or reform schools. Besides being physically segregated, patients find themselves isolated in other ways. They are unable to find or to hold a job, to find friends, or to gain love. Many responsible people, well able to fulfill their needs, do not conform to some of society's generally accepted rules and may superficially resemble psychiatric patients. They may isolate themselves as did Thoreau, but when they wish to return to society, they can do so. Many who seek psychiatric help cannot come close to others or conform to the standards of society no matter how they would like to.

The therapist must have knowledge and understanding about the person who is isolated or different because he cannot properly fulfill his needs. The therapist must accept him as he is at first. An important distinguishing trait of a good psychotherapist is his ability to accept patients uncritically and understand their behavior. He must never be frightened or rebuffed by the patient's behavior no matter how aberrant it is. One way patients test the therapist is by acting irrationally. The therapist must remain steady in the face of unusual behavior, an almost impossible task unless he has had experience working with many different patients under various conditions. All psychiatrists must have a minimum of three years of training as therapists to give them the necessary experience. The patient, recognizing a man who accepts, understands, and is not frightened, moves rapidly toward involvement.

Finally, the therapist must be able to become emotionally involved with each patient. To some extent he must be affected by the patient and his problems and even suffer with him. The therapist who can work with seriously irresponsible people and not be affected by their suffering will never become sufficiently involved to do successful therapy.

Involvement may be attained quickly with patients who are fairly responsible; with more irresponsible patients it takes much longer. The process can be hastened when the patient is in an institution and the therapist can exert some control over his life. In any case, attaining involvement is the essence of therapy. The patient can then begin to face reality, the next step in treatment.

Perhaps two examples from recent, critically acclaimed plays can clarify the kind of involvement which must occur in therapy. The theme of the play *A Man for All Seasons,* by Robert Bolt, is the conflict between Thomas More and King Henry VIII over Henry's decision to divorce Catherine, his first wife, and marry Anne Boleyn. Tired of the older Catherine and infatuated with Anne, Henry excused his decision on the premise that Catherine was unable to provide him with the male heir he needed to insure succession for the Tudors. Thomas More, first a councilor, then the Chancellor of England, refused to state that the king's proposed divorce was legal. More's refusal led ultimately to his execution—justified by false evidence and perjured testimony.

The relationship between More and the king is the model for the ideal therapeutic involvement, even though the outcome was far different from the usual result of therapy. It is cited to show that the sought-for psychiatric involvement is by no means restricted to therapeutic relationships. Many humans become involved in this way. The difference is that ordinary involvements may or may not be purposeful; in psychiatry involvement is always the goal.

Thomas More, the man for all seasons, was by all the definitions in this book a highly responsible man. He lived a life of right and he did not hesitate to act according to his beliefs. Believing strongly in God and the Catholic Church, he was able to perceive that many men, even in the clergy, did little more than mouth the principles he lived by. He rose rapidly in English politics, not because he sought to do so, but because the king prized the qualities of responsibility that he personified. Early in his career he became deeply involved with the king and helped him write a book defending the Catholic position against the Lutheran attack, a defense which Henry completely abandoned in his split with the Church over his divorce of Catherine.

There is no doubt that Henry admired and respected More. His attitude is dramatically demonstrated in the first act when More asks the king, who has the power to divorce Catherine and the acquiescence of many powerful people, why he cares whether or not More consents. The king puts it on a personal level when he replies, "Because you are honest." Knowing that his decision was irresponsible, the king felt a loss of self-worth that could only be restored by More's consent. More would not give it. To protect himself and his family, and hoping that in time the king would see the irresponsibility of his position, More said that he would remain silent rather than state his opinion, publicly or privately, of the king's actions.

If these men had not been involved, the king would not have needed More's support. Because they were deeply involved, the issue could not be avoided. More knew the king well enough to know that it was useless to discuss the irresponsibility; Henry would not change. Discussion of irresponsibility with stubborn patients before they are ready to change only serves to encourage the patient to try to justify his irresponsible position. A therapist who allows this may give the patient false hope, which More would not do. On issues where the king was responsible or might change, they could continue to talk and maintain their relationship; as in therapy, however, nothing is gained by discussing a man's irresponsibility beyond the joint recognition that it exists and that only he can do something about it. A desire to take responsible action is grounds for discussion, of course, but the king had no such desire.

More was executed because the king could not tolerate his refusal to state that the king was right, which was both a public and private deep rebuke. In this involvement, something had to give. As in therapy where there is true involvement, the patient must become more responsible or leave therapy. Hopefully, because of the involvement, he will not leave, so he must give up the irresponsible behavior. Fortunately, few patients take the king's prerogative, although with seriously irresponsible patients threats against the therapist are not uncommon.

Like More with the king, the psychiatrist must become involved with each patient. He must be highly responsible, initially accepting the patient as he is and then withstanding the attempts to get him to condone irresponsibility. Thomas More certainly accepted the king totally in the beginning and hoped he would become more responsible. Only as time passed did More reject the grossly irresponsible act, but even to the end he did not publicly or privately reject the king. Every therapist must be able to do the same.

A happier outcome of the struggle between responsibility and irresponsibility occurs in *The Miracle Worker,* William Gibson's dramatic story of Annie Sullivan's impact on Helen Keller in the first few months of their long relationship. We see the genesis of an involvement which started as a therapeutic relationship and later flowered into deep friendship between two highly responsible people.

When Annie Sullivan arrived in Alabama after an arduous trip from Boston, she was horrified to see how badly her pupil, Helen, behaved, with little effort on the part of anyone to correct her animal-like actions. Rather than take the family attitude of feeling sorry for Helen because she was blind and deaf, Annie felt anguish because Helen, with her handicap, was accepted as capable of nothing. Annie's initial attempts to get involved failed because Helen would always run to her doting parents to gain her irresponsible ends.

Certainly Helen was accepted for what she was; the problem was that no one had understood the need for taking the next step—to continue to accept her but to reject her irresponsible behavior. Annie recognized that unless they could become so deeply involved that Helen would be completely dependent upon Annie alone, there could be no change.

Against much family disapproval, Annie persuaded Captain Keller to allow her to keep Helen alone for two weeks in a small house on the farm. During those two weeks, through love and discipline, Helen began to understand that there was more to living than the life she had known. Annie's will, her strength, her love, and her keen perception that Helen must be taught to fulfill her basic needs, achieved the miracle of Helen Keller.

While the relationship between More and the king resembled

that of patient and therapist in private practice, what developed between Helen and Annie is nearer the relationship necessary for the beginning of therapy in a mental hospital or a correctional school. As delinquents and hospital patients often do, Helen fought the therapist and had to be restrained by force in the beginning. Later, when her needs began to be better fulfilled, the involvement deepened until Annie became the most important person in her life. Therapy would have been unsuccessful if Annie had not been a tough, highly responsible person willing to risk her own meager reputation for what she believed was right. She accepted Helen, not as a poor blind-deaf puppy, but as an intelligent child with high potential who was totally irresponsible. Annie refused to accept Helen's irresponsibility as necessitated or even excused by her handicaps. On the contrary, Annie felt that because of her handicaps Helen needed to excel, and ultimately she did. That their involvement deepened as Helen learned to be more responsible was shown dramatically by her running to Annie when she spoke her first word.

Developing a therapeutic involvement may take anywhere from one interview to several months, depending upon the skill of the therapist, his control over the patient, and the resistance of the patient. Once it occurs, the therapist begins to insist that the patient face the reality of his behavior. He is no longer allowed to evade recognizing what he is doing or his responsibility for it. When the therapist takes this step—and he should start as soon as involvement begins—the relationship deepens because now someone cares enough about the patient to make him face a truth that he has spent his life trying to avoid: *he is responsible for his behavior*. Now, continually confronted with reality by the therapist, he is not allowed to excuse or condone any of his behavior. No reason is acceptable to the therapist for any irresponsible behavior. He confronts the patient with his behavior and asks him to decide whether or not he is taking the responsible course. The patient thus finds a man who cares enough about him to reject behavior which will not help him to fulfill his needs.

In Reality Therapy we are much more concerned with behavior than with attitudes. Once we are involved with the patient, we begin to point out to him the unrealistic aspects of his irresponsible behavior. If the patient wishes to argue that his conception of reality is correct, we must be willing to discuss his opinions, but we must not fail to emphasize that our main interest is his behavior rather than his attitude.

Suppose an adolescent girl has continual temper tantrums over her mother's unwillingness to let her date a certain boy. If in therapy we had attained a good involvement with the girl, we would ask her to try just once to discuss the subject with her mother without losing her temper. She may say there is no point in talking to her mother, that even if she holds her temper, her feelings about the situation will be unchanged. On the other hand, she may agree to take our advice and the whole problem may suddenly disappear, a very common occurrence.

This actually happened and not because we made a magic suggestion, but because the girl had learned a valuable lesson in need fulfillment. *She had become willing to try a new pattern of behavior, regardless of her conviction that it wouldn't work.*

The change had a dramatic effect on the girl's mother. She saw her daughter in a different light. The mother grew calmer, and for the first time the question of dating the boy could be discussed on its merits. The conflict between the mother and daughter began to disappear when they could talk to each other reasonably. As they felt more love for each other and more worthwhile themselves, the problem was quickly solved.

This brief example demonstrates how waiting for attitudes to change stalls therapy whereas changing behavior leads quickly to a change in attitude, which in turn can lead to fulfilling needs and further better behavior. The Negro groups fighting for their civil rights use the same argument. If they wait for the attitude of the people of Mississippi to change, they may wait forever.

Along with the emphasis on behavior and as a continuing part of the involvement, the therapist freely gives praise when the patient acts responsibly and shows disapproval when he does not. The patient demands this judgment, which is a natural expression of faith between two people, as a test of the sincerity of the relationship. The patient rather than the therapist must decide whether or not his behavior is irresponsible and whether he should change it. If a boy thinks that he cannot help stealing cars, no therapy is possible. If a man thinks that it is all right to overeat and be fat, no obesity treatment will work. The skill of therapy is to put the responsibility upon the patient and, after involvement is established, to ask him why he remains in therapy if he is not dissatisfied with his behavior. In private practice, where the patient comes voluntarily, the timing of this question is vital. It must not be asked before the involvement is deep enough to force the patient to stop defending his irresponsible actions rather than leave therapy. Even a skillful therapist may lose a patient if he asks this question too soon. Usually a patient who leaves office therapy under these circumstances will return because of course nothing will change to make his life better. In treatment the skillful therapist does not make the point blatantly; rather, it is implied during the whole process of therapy.

Delinquents or psychotics in custodial institutions may resist therapy. The proper function of any treatment institution is to provide a warm, disciplined atmosphere in which the inmates are required to assess their behavior in terms of responsibility. Institutions which do not do so, whether they bear the label of hospital or reform school, are only prisons. The inmates learn nothing except to deny reality further. As Annie Sullivan did with Helen Keller, the personnel of a good institution may have to compel an inmate to remain in therapy in the beginning. When he discovers that he can fulfill his needs under the pressure of therapy, he learns that what at first seemed to be only force was the concern of the therapist for him. Once involvement is attained, even the most resistant patient will voluntarily stop defending his irresponsibility rather than leave treatment.

As therapy proceeds, the therapist must teach the patient that therapy is not primarily directed toward making him happy. Accepting the premise that people can find happiness only for themselves, the therapist must guide the patient toward understanding that no one can make another person happy for long unless he becomes more responsible. Happiness occurs most often when we are willing to take responsibility for our behavior. Irresponsible people, always seeking to gain happiness without assuming responsibility, find only brief periods of joy, but not the deep-seated satisfaction which accompanies responsible behavior. When they have a problem they may try to ignore it, drown it in alcohol, or rationalize it away—all in an effort to gain brief happiness. When they are finally faced with reality, when they can no longer ignore or rationalize their action, they suffer and run for help. However, the only help that will do any good is that which guides them toward the responsibility they are so steadfastly avoiding.

The therapist who accepts excuses, ignores reality, or allows the patient to blame his present unhappiness on a parent or on an emotional disturbance can usually make his patient feel good temporarily at the price of evading responsibility. He is only giving the patient "psychiatric kicks," which are no different from the brief kicks he may have obtained from alcohol, pills, or sympathetic friends before consulting the psychiatrist. When they fade, as they soon must, the patient with good reason becomes disillusioned with psychiatry.

Plausible as it may seem, we must never delude ourselves into wrongly concluding that unhappiness led to the patient's behavior, that a delinquent child broke the law because he was miserable, and that therefore our job is to make him happy. He broke the law not because he was angry or bored, but because he was irresponsible. The unhappiness is not a cause but a companion to his irresponsible behavior. Is anything gained by giving in to an irresponsible sixteen-year-old boy who says he must have a car to be happy? A host of parents have learned through bitter experience that one cannot purchase happiness for an irresponsible child. A car merely allows the boy to extend the scope and magnitude of his irresponsibility and give him some brief moments of joy before his pattern deteriorates further. A girl who makes herself and her parents miserable because they won't allow her to leave high school to get married usually finds only brief pleasure when her parents bow to her pressure. Among the most unhappy people in our society are young, divorced mothers with two or three children who were too impatient to wait for emotional maturity before marriage.

The reader may wonder what the conversation between patient and doctor consists of if the latter is not interested in the patient's history, his unconscious mind, or even in making him happy. As part of becoming involved the therapist must become interested in and discuss all aspects of the patient's present life. Relating discussion to his behavior whenever possible, we talk about his interests, hopes, fears, opinions, and particularly his values—his own personal ideas of right and wrong. We are interested in him as a person with a wide potential, not just as a patient with problems. In fact, one of the best ways not to become involved is to discuss his problems over and over. Although continually listening to misery is one way of giving the patient sympathy, he soon discovers that with all the talk the therapist can do nothing directly to solve his problems.

We must open up his life, talk about new horizons, expand his range of interests, make him aware of life beyond his difficulties. Anything two people might discuss is grist for therapy: politics, plays, books, movies, sports, hobbies, finances, health, marriage, sex, and religion are all possible topics.

The patient accomplishes two important objectives through these discussions in which he gives his considered opinions to the therapist. First, by testing the opinions of the therapist on many subjects, he discovers that it is possible to maintain, as the therapist must, a responsible attitude toward most facets of life. Because the therapist opens himself to criticism, the patient is able to find out the kind of person on whom he has relied. General discussion provides a good opportunity for the continual testing of the therapist that is characteristic of the beginning of therapy. No one will become more responsible unless he is thoroughly convinced that he is involved with a responsible therapist.

Second, the patient develops an increased sense of self-worth in the process of parrying his convictions and values with a trusted, respected person. The therapist relates the discussions to what the patient is doing now, confronting him with the reality of what he does as compared to what he says. Sessions which do not bear directly on the patient's problems are not wasted as long as they relate to his growing awareness that he is a part of the world and that perhaps he can cope with it. *When values, standards, and responsibility are in the background, all discussion is relevant to therapy.* Continually stressing responsibility is artificial.

The therapist now directly, but skillfully, interweaves a discussion of the patient's strong points. Discussing those areas in which he acts responsibly, we show how they can be expanded. We never sympathize with, or excuse him for anything he does, nor do we let him excuse himself. We never agree that his irresponsibility is justified no matter how much he may have suffered at the hands of others.

Because the patient must gain responsibility right now, we always focus on the present. The past has certainly contributed to what he is now, but we cannot change the past, only the present. Recounting his history in the hope that he will learn from his mistakes rarely proves successful and should be avoided. From past mistakes the patient learns only that he knew better at the time, yet still did not act on his knowledge. It may be interesting to talk about past errors with friends or family, but it is a waste of time to discuss them with the therapist. The present, the right now, is the critical task, not the easy job of recounting his historical irresponsibility and looking for excuses. Why become involved with the irresponsible person he was? We want to become involved with the responsible person we know he can be.

In Reality Therapy emotions and happiness are never divorced from behavior. Gaining insight into the unconscious thinking which accompanies aberrant behavior is not an objective; excuses for deviant behavior are not accepted and one's history is not made more important than one's present life. We never blame others for the patient's irresponsibility or censure mother, father, or anyone deeply involved with the patient no matter how irresponsible they are or were. The patient cannot change them; he can only learn better ways to live with them or without them. We never encourage hostility or acting out irresponsible impulses, for that only compounds the problem. We never condemn society. If a Negro, for example, feels limited by the white society, he must still take a responsible course of action. Blind hatred of his oppressors gains nothing for him or anyone else in a similar position.

In Reality Therapy, therefore, we rarely ask why. Our usual question is *What? What* are you doing—not, *why* are you doing it? Why implies that the reasons for the patient's behavior make a difference in therapy, but they do not. The patient will himself search for reasons; but until he has become more responsible he will not be able to act differently, even when he knows why. All the reasons in the world for why he drinks will not lead an alcoholic to stop. Change will occur only when he fulfills his needs more satisfactorily. Then the reasons become unimportant because the need to drink will have disappeared. All aberrant behavior is either an attempt to evade or an inability to take the responsibility of doing right, of fulfilling our basic needs. Alcoholics Anonymous, for example, is successful in many instances because it fulfills the needs of the alcoholic, but first he has to give up all evasions and admit he is an alcoholic. The therapist's job is to point out the reality of what the patient is doing now, not to search with him for the "why" that he will always grasp in an effort not to change. Thus, in our effort toward helping him gain more conscious responsible control over what he does, we adhere closely to the reality of the present.

When the patient admits that his behavior is irresponsible, the last phase of therapy—relearning—begins. Actually no definite change in therapy occurs; relearning is merged into the whole treatment. The patient must rely on the therapist's experience to help him learn better ways of behavior. When he can do so, when the young delinquent learns the value of working and experiences the good feelings that accompany responsible action, therapy is approaching an end. It is only a matter of time until the patient, with his newly acquired responsible behavior, begins to fulfill his needs. He finds new relationships, more satisfying involvements, and needs the therapist less. Visits become less frequent as both therapist and patient are aware of the approaching end. Parting is a pleasant time, but it is not necessarily final nor should it be. The stress and strain of living may cause the patient to return, but not for more than brief relearning periods. Once the specific situation is responsibly handled, the patient leaves again.

Although people familiar with psychotherapy will have little difficulty understanding Reality Therapy from the previous discussion, other readers might not see clearly what we do. Tape-recording and transcribing verbatim have been tried, but in my experience little has been learned. Even observing a series of sessions through a concealed window would reveal little because the involvement, the relationship which develops between therapist and patient, can only be viewed as a whole. Breaking it into small segments is as misleading as plucking a piece of a jigsaw puzzle from the box and studying it. One might learn everything about the piece, yet little of the whole picture. Only after all the pieces are put together can the full picture be appreciated. Certainly there are dramatic moments in Reality Therapy and certainly what is said in each session is important, but primary importance must be given to the whole process, during which the patient gradually changes his behavior from irresponsible to responsible. Although patients recognize this change, they are rarely able to pinpoint exactly when it began or what caused it. All they know is that their whole attitude is different.

Recently Margaret, a patient who had been coming once a week for a year, asked to come every other week because she felt so much better able to cope with the world than she had in the past. When I agreed that she was ready to come less often, she tried to put into words what had happened that led to her doing so much better. She found it difficult, saying "I'm the same, but I'm different. I've gotten no great insights. (She had been in traditional therapy looking for these insights for two years before coming to me.) We seemed to have talked very little of what was important, but now I feel much better, and many things which I couldn't do, I am now able to do well." She asked me if I knew what had happened. I told her that we talked about what was really important, that I had always pointed out reality, and that I had never accepted her irrationality, promiscuity, or depression as excusable ways of coping with her world. Rather than looking for *why* she was the way she was, I had made sure that she knew *what* she was doing. Margaret was motivated to change and able to change *because* nothing dramatic had been dredged from her subconscious, *because* her irresponsible past had been left alone, and *because* her fits of depression and promiscuous acting-out had not been excessively discussed. The issues in center stage in usual therapy had been side issues in Reality Therapy. Emphasized were her daily behavior, *what she did* rather than what she felt, and whether she could do better. Because I refused to change my approach when she related her checkered past and erratic present, she was able to become involved with me, sensing that for once in her life she was with someone who seriously expected her to act better and who was not afraid to let her know his expectation whether or not it might upset her.

There were, of course, some emotional outbursts, threats to end everything, to leave town, to quit her job, to run home to her mother, or to go back to her family in New York, all really threats to leave therapy. In response to her threats, I asked, "How will this action help you?" I could not help her work out her problems unless she stayed in therapy. She was testing me. Would I become involved with her misery, or would I continue to show confidence in her ability to do better? Through such give and take we became sufficiently involved for her to begin to fulfill her needs. I told her to move from a shabby furnished room into a nice apartment and buy a few decent pieces of furniture. "Even if you feel bad," I suggested, "you don't have to live so badly." When she mentioned a possible promotion, I told her to work for it rather than to look around constantly for excuses to quit. Eventually she did make a menial office job into a considerably better, even desirable job.

No longer frantically scrambling for love, she is waiting for good friendships to build, and slowly accomplishing a few things well. No one would describe her as happy because she hasn't that much to be happy about, but she is no longer painfully unhappy. Her depressions come much less often, her psychosomatic gastro-intestinal complaints have stopped, and she has weeks when she feels fairly comfortable. Even though she is a divorced woman with few friends in a strange city, she is gaining the strength to live a new life, finding not happiness perhaps but periods of peace, a new experience for her.

Although she said, "Nothing really happened," we both know that all of therapy is what happened. It is this "all"—the involvement, the facing of reality, the learning better ways—which was almost impossible for her to put into words, yet it is this "all" which is therapy.

Perhaps another example will help clarify what happens in therapy. Rob came to me from a university psychiatric clinic where he had been in treatment for a year because he was failing in school, feeling depressed, and complaining bitterly that his home situation was miserable and that he felt lost in the world. The resident psychiatrist was leaving, and the social worker to whom the case was referred asked me if I could see him at a reduced fee; she recognized his need for a long period of therapy with one therapist, which the clinic was unable to provide.

At nineteen Rob was despondent because he was failing in his freshman year at college, he hadn't the vaguest idea where he was heading, and he felt that life was empty. Blaming his failure on his mother and stepfather, in therapy he had hoped to find out why he was the way he was, and counted upon gaining the understanding that could change his life. After a year of conventional treatment he thought of therapy as an intellectual exercise rather than an opportunity to become involved with someone whom he cared about and who cared about him. His intellectual approach had served to keep him from getting close enough to anyone to become involved.

At our first meeting, I told Rob that I would see him once a week and that we would work on his school difficulties first. This brief statement told him that his problems were not insoluble and that I was interested in working with him. The involvement started with this simple but necessary statement. An agreement to see the patient and to help him solve his problems is basic to beginning therapy, and in every case described in this book, the promise is made in some form. Even with a patient who is out of contact with reality, as in a mental hospital, or violently resistant to psychiatric treatment, as a delinquent adolescent often is, this much has to be stated and then carried out with force if necessary. Whether he came to therapy voluntarily or was brought there forcibly the patient must hear expressed the idea, *"I will see you until you can become better able to fulfill your needs."*

Next we had to settle on the fee. Although Rob's mother told him that she could pay ten dollars a week, I questioned her ability to do so, knowing the family's financial condition. Could he pay half himself? He was working in the college library and earning more than twelve dollars a week. Would he be willing to pay five dollars toward his therapy? By agreeing he took several further steps toward becoming involved. First, through my suggestion, he could be less dependent upon his mother which, at age nineteen, he certainly desired to be. In turn she would be less burdened with him, which she wanted but which she was afraid of because she didn't want him to leave her, either physically or emotionally. Insecure in her third marriage, she was not ready to let go of him. Sharing the cost was beneficial to both of them; my suggestion had set the stage for him to fulfill his needs independently of her.

The therapist cannot get involved with the patient unless he is different from everyone else in the patient's life. Rob's failures were symptomatic of his lack of need fulfillment; no one in the past had been successful in getting properly involved with him. But his failures were the best he had been able to do, they seemed important to him, and he wanted to tell me about them in detail. In doing so he was trying to gain my sympathy. If I had listened then to all this "psychiatric garbage," as I like to call an unhappy past, I would have necessarily assumed a superior role. A person feels inferior when he tells of his failures and misfortunes unless he is closely involved with the listener. Rob and I were not nearly close enough at this time, so I did not fall into the common psychiatric trap in which the patient, through his miserable life's history, degrades himself before the therapist.

Instead I took the initiative. I asked him to tell me his plan (a favorite Reality Therapy question). Asking him for his plan tells him that he should have a plan, or at least start thinking of one, putting him in a position where, instead of unburdening his troubles, he should begin some constructive thinking about what he is doing right now and about his future. He reacted typically by asking, "What plan, what do you have in mind?" I said, "Well, here you are at college. You must have a plan, or a goal, some place you are heading for, some idea of how to get there." At least he might have an aspiration, something we could discuss. My open question does not tie him to a concrete plan; rather I was telling him that he could bare his aspirations to me. I would listen and help direct him toward fulfillment of these aspirations if in reality they were at all possible. Still he resisted. He wanted to talk about his mother, his hated stepfather, his hated little brother, and his hated previous stepfather. These subjects were easy for him, they excused his failures, but they would lead nowhere. I reassured him by saying that we could talk about his family at any time. I wanted now to talk about what he had in mind for himself, what he could do which would lead to a satisfactory future. I wanted the focus upon him, not upon others, because only he could solve his problems.

Although this unexpected shift in attitude from that of the previous therapist, who had listened to his miseries, was hard for him to comprehend, he quickly recognized that I cared very much about him and what he could do. He began to express some thoughts that he had not dared to voice in the past: what he might really do if he could overcome the obstacles he thought were in his way, particularly the failure he felt he was in college. I said, "Forget the past. Grades can be improved, courses can be retaken. But even assuming," I continued, "all your grades were A's and B's, where would you want to go?" He had said before, "I don't know, I really don't know." But this answer was not the truth. Although he did want to be an educated professional man, he had spent so much time failing, groping, and feeling sorry for his condition and for others like him (in his pseudo-liberal compassion for others, which really is feeling sorry for himself), so much time blaming the world and generally wallowing in his own inadequacy and misery, that he was surprised to find that he seemed almost afraid to hope. He was not involved enough with responsible people to have a plan or even to express a hope for fear that the actual expression might blow his hope away. I told him, "If you can't come up with a plan yourself, we'll start by figuring one out together. You think about it and I will too."

The stage was now set for therapy. We could talk about almost anything because any subject might lead to a plan for him. He was young, intelligent, physically in good condition, in a good college, and there were no serious restrictions to what he might become. He had rarely talked to a responsible adult, and never to one with whom he was involved, about the world in general. We found much to talk about; in addition to many general subjects we talked about what he was doing now at school and at home. The conversation concerning his personal life was always directed toward what he was doing rather than his opinions about what was happening to him because of his mother, stepfather, or his professors.

Our conversations were not dramatic. They were earnest discussions between two people, one of whom had problems to solve because he was irresponsible, the other, a responsible person interested in helping him solve these problems. As part of the discussions, I told him about my early college days, what I did, where I failed, where I succeeded, and what I learned in the process. I was not putting myself in his shoes or being condescending, I was telling him honestly what had happened to me and how I arrived where I am. He was interested and he appreciated my openness and my warmth. The involvement grew, and as it did, I began to read his papers, to discuss his homework, and to talk over his tests. I also suggested that he seek out his stepfather, get to know him, try to see his point of view, and appreciate his problems in trying to head a family with two jealous stepsons. Acting on my suggestion, he was able to talk to his stepfather and began to see him in a better light. They have since become very close. As his life improved, I was able to point out what he was doing to produce the changes that we both recognized.

For the first time he began searching for a specific goal. It was not surprising that he brought up medicine, although he immediately said that it would be impossible for him to become a doctor. He could never pass the technical subjects—chemistry, physics, math, or biology—nor could he afford to go to medical school even if, by some miracle, he were accepted. He thought of himself as a liberal arts student, a thinker, an appreciator of intellectual discussion, the social sciences, and the fine arts. Technical subjects had specific answers, and he was afraid of situations that called for being specific. It had never occurred to him that technical subjects might be easy if one approached them reasonably and without fear; in a sense they were easier than liberal arts subjects that did not have definite answers. In high school he only took those scientific subjects required for graduation. As a college freshman he almost failed chemistry, finally dropping the course. As his plans began to form, we continued to discuss various possibilities. Agreeing that medicine was a remote goal, I nevertheless suggested that we shouldn't rule it out. He said he would like to work with people, perhaps pointing toward social work by majoring in sociology. Generally approving of this plan, I added that medical schools were searching just as much for candidates educated in the social sciences as for those trained in the physical and biological sciences. Perhaps he might satisfy the minimum requirements for medicine while majoring in sociology. This was the final plan. Knowing where he was going, he lost his fear of technical subjects and school was no longer a problem. He was graduated with better than a B average.

In the beginning of his senior year, two years after we had started therapy, Rob began to discuss his real father, now living in the East, whom he had not seen since infancy. He obtained his address through his mother and together we composed a letter. Almost immediately he received a warm and encouraging answer. Through his successful involvement with me he was able to try to become involved with his father, someone whom he felt he needed very much. For the next three months several letters passed back and forth. One day, with no warning whatsoever, he received a letter from his uncle (his father's brother) saying that his father's wife had died from an operation following heart surgery, leaving his father with two small children, Rob's half-brother and half-sister, whom he had never seen. His father, unable to cope with this responsibility, committed suicide a week after his wife died. The uncle, who had taken custody of the children, had written Rob, the only other close relative. Rob was shaken. He asked me what to do, and when I pointed out reality, he was strong enough to agree with my evaluation of the situation. Although he originally felt he should have been able to do something to avoid his father's taking his life, I was able to reassure him that there was nothing he could have done. I did, however, point out that he did have an obligation to his half-brother and half-sister. In his own immediate feelings of guilt and self-pity, it took a little while before he realized that he should do something for them. When he recognized his responsibility to them, he snapped out of his depression and went to work harder than ever. He wrote to the children and to his uncle, told them of his interest, and received encouraging letters from all of them. Even the difficult reality of his father's death gave him an opportunity to gain self-worth, rather than use the tragedy as an excuse to lapse into his former irresponsible ways.

Soon after this tragic occurrence therapy ended. Surprising to him but not to me, he was accepted by every medical school to which he applied. His stepfather is now doing better financially and his mother continues to work; enthusiastic over his achievements, they are able to help him through medical school. Although I hear from him only occasionally, this year he did call to say he was elected president of his class in medical school.

In summary, then, our basic job as therapists is to become involved with the patient and then get him to face reality. When confronted with reality by the therapist with whom he is involved, he is forced again and again to decide whether or not he wishes to take the responsible path. Reality may be painful, it may be harsh, it may be dangerous, but it changes slowly. All any man can hope to do is to struggle with it in a responsible way by doing right and enjoying the pleasure or suffering the pain that may follow.

2 | The Differences between Reality Therapy and Conventional Therapy

Having described Reality Therapy in the previous chapter, I now wish to make clear the major differences, both in theory and practice, between Reality Therapy and what is widely accepted as conventional psychotherapy. Conventional therapy, based either strictly or loosely upon the psychoanalytic beliefs and teachings of Sigmund Freud, is taught in almost every major college and university in the United States and Canada. Whether it is practiced in an orthodox, Freudian setting in a Park Avenue psychoanalyst's office or in a loosely structured college counseling service, it embodies the following:

1. Conventional psychiatry believes firmly that mental illness exists, that people who suffer from it can be meaningfully classified, and that attempts should be made to treat them according to the diagnostic classification.

2. Conventional psychiatry holds that an essential part of treatment is probing into the patient's past life—searching for the psychological roots of his problem because once the patient clearly understands these roots he can use his understanding to change his attitude toward life. From this change in attitude he can then develop more effective patterns of living which will solve his psychological difficulties.

3. Conventional psychiatry maintains that the patient must transfer to the therapist attitudes he held or still holds toward important people in his past life, people around whom his problems started. Using this concept, called transference, the therapist relives with the patient his past difficulties and then explains to him how he is repeating the same inadequate behavior with the therapist. The patient, through the therapist's interpretations of the transference behavior, gains insight into his past. His newly attained insight allows him to give up his old attitudes and to learn to relate to people in a better way, solving his problems.

4. Conventional psychotherapy, even in superficial counseling, emphasizes that if the patient is to change he must gain understanding and insight into his unconscious mind. Unconscious mental conflicts are considered more important than conscious problems; making the patient aware of them through the interpretation of transference, dreams, and free associations, and through educated psychiatric guessing, is necessary if therapy is to succeed.

5. Necessarily accompanying the conviction that mental illness exists, conventional psychiatry scrupulously avoids the problem of morality, that is, whether the patient's behavior is right or wrong. Deviant behavior is considered a product of the mental illness, and the patient should not be held morally responsible because he is considered helpless to do anything about it. Once the illness is cured through the procedures described in Points 2, 3, and 4, the patient will then be able to behave according to the rules of society.

6. Teaching people to behave better is not considered an important part of therapy in conventional psychiatry, which holds the patients will learn better behavior themselves once they understand both the historical and unconscious sources of their problems.

Using these six essential convictions as a basis for both psychiatric theory and practice, conventional psychiatry may appear in many forms from simple counseling through non-directive therapy to orthodox psychoanalysis, but in every situation almost everyone who does therapy in the United States and Canada today would concur with these six criteria. Although some people might place more emphasis upon one than another, usually they stand unchallenged.

Reality Therapy in both theory and practice challenges the validity of each of these basic beliefs. In this chapter I would like to examine each concept in detail and show how Reality Therapy differs from the therapy which has been so widely accepted for so many years.

Before examining each concept individually, one over-all difference between Reality Therapy and conventional psychiatry must be emphasized. This is the difference between the involvement necessary for Reality Therapy and the involvement necessary for conventional therapy. In Reality Therapy achieving the proper involvement is absolutely essential. Although involvement is also important in conventional therapy, it is emphasized less and it is much different from the involvement in Reality Therapy. The conventional therapist is taught to remain as impersonal and objective as possible and not to become involved with the patient as a separate and important person in the patient's life. Rather, he is to strive for the transference relationship briefly described under Point 3 above.

The way Reality Therapy differs from conventional therapy on each of the six points to be discussed contributes to the major difference in involvement. The six points may be considered briefly from the standpoint of involvement.

1. Because we do not accept the concept of mental illness, the patient cannot become involved with us as a mentally ill person who has no responsibility for his behavior.

2. Working in the present and toward the future, we do not get involved with the patient's history because we can neither change what happened to him nor accept the fact that he is limited by his past.

3. We relate to patients as ourselves, not as transference figures.

4. We do not look for unconscious conflicts or the reasons for them. A patient cannot become involved with us by excusing his behavior on the basis of unconscious motivations.

5. We emphasize the morality of behavior. We face the issue of right and wrong which we believe solidifies the involvement, in contrast to conventional psychiatrists who do not make the distinction between right and wrong, feeling it would be detrimental to attaining the transference relationship they seek.

6. We teach patients better ways to fulfill their needs. The proper involvement will not be maintained unless the patient is helped to find more satisfactory patterns of behavior. Conventional therapists do not feel that teaching better behavior is a part of therapy.

In the detailed discussion to follow, it will be clear that each of the six points of difference between Reality Therapy and conventional psychiatry contributes to the difference between the way we become involved with our patients and how conventional psychiatrists relate to theirs. With the over-all difference of involvement in mind, let us examine in detail the six major beliefs of conventional psychiatry and compare them to the theory and practice of Reality Therapy.

First, and very important from a treatment standpoint, both the theory and practice of Reality Therapy are incompatible with the prevalent, widely accepted concept of mental illness. We believe that this concept, the belief that people can and do suffer from some specific, diagnosable, treatable mental illness, analogous to a specific, diagnosable, treatable physical illness, is inaccurate and that this inaccuracy is a major road block to proper psychiatric treatment. Our scientific and lay literature are both filled with the idea that anyone who behaves and thinks in a way unacceptable to the majority of the society is mentally ill or, in popular terms, "sick." Every conventional psychiatric approach to the treatment of these people (whom we have described in Chapter 1 as irresponsible because they are unable to fulfill their needs) is based upon the belief that they are suffering from mental illness, a concept as prevalent to our culture as the flatness of the earth was to the Middle Ages.

Those who believe in mental illness assume incorrectly that something definite is wrong with the patient which causes him to be the way he is. Most psychiatrists believe that the patient was all right at one time and then fell victim to a series of unhappy life experiences which now cause his deviant behavior. When these experiences are exposed and resolved through conventional psychotherapy, the mentally ill person will recover in much the same way that the physically ill person recovers from a strep throat when the penicillin kills the streptococcus. We believe this concept misleads the doctor, the patient, and those concerned with him into the false belief that the doctor's job is to treat some definite condition, after which the patient will get well. This attitude was graphically illustrated by a patient whom I treated some years ago, an imposing woman who sat down, looked directly at me, and stated in all sincerity, "I'm here, Doctor. Do psychiatry!"

We believe that throughout their lives people constantly strive to fulfill their needs. Any time in their lives when they are unsuccessful in doing so, they behave unrealistically. Very strong people may behave unrealistically only under extreme stress; others may do so under less adverse conditions, sometimes from an early age, indicating a lifelong inability to form a satisfying relationship with a responsible person.

Those who believe in mental illness try to remove some specific internal psychological cause (the often heard "root of the problem"), which they believe is responsible for the patient's present deviant behavior. Conventional psychiatry, almost without fail, relates this cause to instances in his previous life when the patient was unable to cope with stress. We believe that there is no noxious psychological causative agent to remove. *Our job is to help the patient help himself to fulfill his needs right now.*

If there is a medical analogy which applies to psychiatric problems, it is not illness but weakness. While illness can be cured by removing the causative agent, weakness can be cured only by strengthening the existing body to cope with the stress of the world, large or small as this stress may be.

By dispensing with the idea of mental illness and calling a man irresponsible, and then describing how he is irresponsible, Reality Therapy defines the situation much more precisely. Using the latter description, it is apparent that the cause of the psychiatric patient's condition is different from that of a patient with a physical illness, who is more truly the victim of forces outside himself. Regardless of past circumstances, the psychiatric patient must develop the strength to take the responsibility to fulfill his needs satisfactorily. Treatment, therefore, is not to give him understanding of past misfortunes which caused his "illness," but to help him to function in a better way right now.

Philosophically, as well as practically, from the patient's standpoint there is a world of difference between being cured of an illness and helping oneself. With typhoid fever, one may be as motivated as possible and still die unless some capable physician gives the proper medical treatment. A car-stealing juvenile delinquent, however, treated by a psychiatrist for years on the basis of mental illness, will not change as long as he is allowed to play the misunderstood or mistreated child who doesn't understand all that has happened to him. He and all other irresponsible people now wrongly labeled "mentally ill" must clearly understand that they must help themselves regardless of what has happened to them in the past (and we should be the last to deny that they have suffered). As long as the mental illness concept prevails and patients continue to see themselves as the recipients of help, we will make little progress in psychiatry. With the hazy conception that most patients and their families have of mental illness, the responsibility for change lies less with them than with the treating agency—be it doctor, social worker, correctional institution, or hospital.

Psychiatrists discovered long ago that as much as they would like to follow the medical parallel and cure the patient of his brain disease, they were unable to do so because no brain pathology existed. Instead of giving up the illness concept, psychiatrists seized on the discovery of unconscious conflicts as the cause of mental illness. It was the conflicts which caused patients to be the way they are, mentally ill. Patients are led on long, expensive trips back through their childhood, often discovering that mother was the cause of it all. Once the patient is helped to wrest his childhood resentments against mother from his unconscious mind, cure is theoretically in sight.

For example, an obese young woman who has a compulsive overeating problem may find out through psychotherapy that her mother wanted a more beautiful daughter. Because obesity in a young woman is never desirable, she overeats in order to avoid facing the truth that her mother would reject her even if she were slim. She can accept the mother's rejection because she is indeed fat and unattractive, perhaps so much so that her mother and others may have given her sympathy, if not acceptance. In traditional therapy, being accepted as mentally ill and having learned why, the patient will attempt to throw herself upon the therapist. Learning from him that the source of the problem is past and present unresolved conflict with her mother, she continues to eat, her appetite undiminished by this knowledge. This not uncommon situation, where the unchanging fat and miserable patient damns her mother for years in psychotherapy, has discredited psychiatry in the minds of many people. Under these too familiar circumstances, where the mental illness is accepted and the cause is sought and discovered to be outside herself (in this case her mother's rejection), the patient is relieved of the necessary responsibility for her part in the therapy. The fat girl's only chance of being helped is to learn that she is irresponsible, not that she is mentally ill, and that her unattractiveness is important primarily to her. Her mother is only an excuse for her irresponsibility. To help this girl we must scrupulously avoid giving her excuses for the way she is, but rather help her give up excusing her inability to fill her needs and guide her toward the reality that she must fulfill them regardless of her mother.

Also misleading but an important part of the mental illness concept is the use of psychiatric diagnoses to label a wide variety of "mental illnesses." The purpose of diagnosis is to select proper treatment. If we diagnose that a headache is caused by a brain tumor, a logical sequence of treatment is suggested. The treatment, which often includes brain surgery, is far different from the treatment that might be given to a severe headache caused by eyestrain or alcoholic hangover. Where treatment logically and necessarily follows diagnosis, correct diagnosis is vital; in the case of so-called mental illnesses, however, treatment by any one doctor, whether psychoanalyst or Reality Therapist, is essentially the same. Psychotherapy lacks the specific and individual treatment which follows the diagnosis of scarlet fever, syphilis, or malaria. Even where there is no specific treatment, as in the common cold, the correct diagnosis hopefully will avoid improper treatment with antibiotics and other detrimental medications.

Using Reality Therapy there is no essential difference in the treatment of various psychiatric problems. As will be explained in later chapters, the treatment of psychotic veterans is almost exactly the same as the treatment of delinquent, adolescent girls. The particular manifestation of irresponsibility (the diagnosis) has little relationship to the treatment. From our standpoint, all that needs to be diagnosed is whether the patient is suffering from irresponsibility, no matter with what behavior he expresses it, or from an organic illness.

Under the heading of "mentally ill" are numerous diagnoses such as schizophrenic, neurotic, depressed, sociopathic, and psychosomatic, all describing some kind of irresponsible behavior. From Chapter 1 we have learned that all these various terms only describe the best the patient has been able to manage in his effort to fulfill his needs. The psychotic patient who believes he is Jesus Christ seems very different from a man with a stomach ulcer, but we should not be fooled by appearances. Like the blind men's descriptions of the elephant, each variety of irresponsible behavior seems much different from all others. Irresponsibility, however, is as basic to the various kinds of behavior as the elephant is basic to his trunk, tail, or legs, and it is the irresponsibilty, the whole elephant, which must be treated.

Unfortunately for taxpayers as well as patients, almost all teaching of psychiatry, psychology, and social work follows traditional thinking that considers the diagnosis of mental illness to be essential to successful treatment. Millions of dollars are spent annually in an attempt to diagnose types of mental illness in the vain hope that the diagnosis will be helpful in treatment. It is pathetically common to hear young psychiatric residents argue whether a certain patient is neurotic because he fears to leave the house, or psychotic because he imagines that an unseen enemy will attack him if he steps outside the door. In either case he suffers from the inability to fulfill his needs. Whether he is afraid of reality (conventionally described as neurotic) or denies reality (psychotic) makes little difference in his life and no difference in treatment. The argument over labels helps no one. Conventional psychiatry wastes too much time arguing over how many diagnoses can dance at the end of a case history, time better spent treating the ever-present problem of irresponsibility.

Necessarily closely related to eliminating the concept of mental illness is the somewhat more radical idea of dispensing with any major inquiry into the patient's past history, ordinarily considered as essential to psychiatry as the scalpel is to the surgeon. Both professional and lay people often ask us, "How can there be any therapy if the therapist does not probe deeply into the patient's past life and uncover each twist and turn?" Light must be cast on each dark corner in the patient's previous life or you cannot help him. The most frustrated critics ask what the patient and the psychiatrist talk about if case history is eliminated from the discussion. Those who read and understood Chapter 1 will realize that *although what has happened to a person may be important as information contributing to developing psychological generalizations* (such as perhaps finding out that boys who have poor relationships with their fathers are more apt to become homosexual), this information has little to do with therapy. Studies of how to raise children to be more responsible are valuable, but finding out how poorly a patient was raised will never change his upbringing. The most complete history possible, perhaps a sound motion picture of the patient's whole life plus a tape recording of every unconscious thought, would be no more helpful in treating a patient than a short description of his present problem. The history merely details ad infinitum the patient's unsuccessful attempts to fulfill his needs. In the end we always discover that right now the patient lacks involvement with a responsible fellow human and that this lack has probably occurred throughout most if not all of his life. In his attempt to fulfill his needs without this essential person he has denied or distorted reality, leading to the present situation in which he is not able to fulfill his needs. The necessity to have a good relationship with a responsible person in order to fulfill one's needs was emphasized in Chapter 1 and need not be repeated here.

Without denying that the patient had an unsatisfactory past, we find that to look for what went wrong does not help him. What good comes from discovering that you are afraid to assert yourself because you had a domineering father? Both patient and therapist can be aware of this historical occurrence, they can discuss it in all of its ramifications for years, but the knowledge will not help the patient assert himself now. In fact, in our experience the more he knows why he cannot assert himself, the less inclined he will be to do so because he now understands that self-assertion is psychologically painful. Most patients will then lean on the psychiatrist, saying, "Now that I know why I can't assert myself, what will make me lose the fear?" The psychiatrist's reply is necessarily weak, "You don't have to be afraid because your father is no longer in the picture." It would be wonderful if therapy were that simple, that knowing the root of the fear would allow the patient to become unafraid.

For Reality Therapy it makes little difference what relationship the patient had with his father. We want to know what is going on now in all aspects of his life. When the patient tells all the details of his past to the therapist, he overemphasizes his inadequacy to the point where it is difficult for him to believe that the therapist can really accept him. Attaining involvement is hampered because involvement can start only on the solid ground of our being able to accept him as he is right now. As therapists, however, we do find it helpful to find out how long his current problem has been going on, not for historical information but to help us gauge whether he will need brief or more extended therapy. For example, if a young patient is failing in school, we might want to know how long he has been failing. If it has been going on for a long time, attaining involvement will be more difficult and therapy will be more intense and take longer than if it is a recent occurrence. We don't have to know the detailed history of his previous failures or his life during those times. The details of his life now, of his present failures, are the material we need.

The conventional psychiatrist depends far too much on the ability of the patient to change his attitude and ultimately his behavior through gaining insight into his unconscious conflicts and inadequacies. In Reality Therapy we emphasize behavior; we do not depend upon insight to change attitudes because in many cases it never will. Once we become involved with a patient and teach him new ways of behavior (as described in Chapter 1) his attitude will change regardless of whether or not he understands his old ways, and then his new attitude will help promote further behavioral change. What starts the process, however, is *an initial change in behavior,* and it is toward this that the therapist must work.

Conventional psychiatrists, led by Freud, have also learned that insight derived from the past is not by itself an effective instrument for change. They have, therefore, developed another concept through which they implement the insight gained through a study of the past. This concept, called *transference,* is an attempt to tie the insight more closely to the present and hopefully make it more useful to the patient.

Although a conventional psychiatrist tries to stay personally uninvolved with the patient during therapy, he certainly does not avoid involvement completely. Instead of a single, intense, personal involvement of doctor with patient, he attempts to gain a series of involvements such as mother to patient, father to patient, brother to patient, teacher to patient, and employer to patient. He does so, according to Reality Therapy, in the mistaken belief that the patient must re-experience in therapy his attitudes toward the important people in his life, past and present. Using transference, the conventional psychiatrist does not tell the patient that he is afraid to assert himself because his father treated him harshly. Instead, he goes halfway toward becoming personally involved with the patient by saying, "You are treating me as if I were your father and blaming your failure to assert yourself upon me." Ironically, the patient is indeed blaming his failure to assert himself upon the psychiatrist, but not because the psychiatrist is like his father. It is because of the difficulty of becoming involved with a therapist who, instead of establishing a close personal relationship with the patient in his own capacity, sometimes plays the role of someone else and sometimes acts as himself.

Psychiatric patients are not seeking to repeat unsuccessful involvements past or present; they are looking for a satisfying human involvement through which they can fulfill their needs now. In conventional therapy an involvement that can benefit the patient may occur if therapy lasts long enough because the patient will eventually relate to the psychiatrist as himself no matter how the psychiatrist protests at the time that he is acting as someone else. The psychiatrist must reject the untherapeutic concept of transference, relate to the patient as a new and separate person with whom the patient can become involved, and through the new involvement teach him to fulfill his needs in the real world of the present.

Closely allied to transference is the concept of the unconscious.

Conventional psychiatry contends that the unconscious motivation is highly important and that for successful therapy the patient must become aware of previously unconscious reasons for the way he behaves. In the transference relationship the therapist is able to point out behavior and thought processes that the patient was not aware of. Besides the transference, he uses projective tests, free associations, dream analysis, and slips of the tongue. These methods all give the therapist insight into the patient's unconscious mind, but they do not help therapy.

Certainly patients, like everyone else, have reasons of which they may be unaware for behaving the way they do. Talking in one's sleep, slips of the tongue, phobias, and compulsions are examples of behavior obviously based upon unconscious mental processes. But we are doing therapy, not research into the cause of human behavior, and we have found that knowledge of cause has nothing to do with therapy. Patients have been treated with conventional psychiatry until they know the unconscious reason for every move they make, but they still do not change because knowing the reason does not lead to fulfilling needs. It is wishful thinking to believe that a man will give up a phobia once he understands either its origin or the current representation of its origin in the transference relationship. He continues to have the phobia because of some *present* irresponsible behavior that may or may not be directly related to the origin of the phobia. If we examine his present life in detail, we will find behavior *of which he is fully conscious* that does not lead to fulfilling his needs. When we help him through Reality Therapy to act in ways that will fulfill his needs, his phobia will disappear. Emphasis upon the unconscious sidetracks the main issue of the patient's irresponsibility and gives him another excuse to avoid facing reality. We cannot emphasize enough that delving into a man's unconscious mind is detrimental to therapy.

The following examples and those in later chapters, in which the successful practice of Reality Therapy with many different kinds of patients is described in detail, clearly show the detrimental effect that utilizing material from the unconscious processes has upon therapy.

First, there is the common case of a man who cannot love. The conventional therapist accepts the patient as being unable to love because he is blocked owing to unconscious conflicts against loving. The reasoning might be, "All women are to him like his mother, so to love a woman becomes incest. By avoiding all love he avoids what is to him a tabooed situation." The patient is considered helpless to change until he gains the knowledge that his feelings toward his present female companion need not be the same as those toward his mother. The patient can now justify his inability to love prior to treatment. As treatment progresses and he still cannot love, the conventional therapist would merely look for deeper blocks, not realizing that the patient's present inability to love may have been reinforced by what he has learned in therapy. Although his inability to fulfill his needs is excused, he continues to suffer because understanding his condition in no way increases his ability to get closer to people who are able to love. Understanding the obstacle does not produce a change in his behavior: that happens only through learning better and more responsible ways to act now. Unfortunately, once he learns about an unconscious obstacle that can justify his behavior, he uses it as an excuse not to change. He is even less able than before to get close to others because he now has a psychiatric reason, reinforced by the prestige of the psychiatrist. Avoiding his present responsibility by escaping into the past, he has become weaker, not stronger, through therapy. We do not deny that at one time he had incestuous feelings; now, however, his needs can be fulfilled only if he faces what he is doing now, what is happening right now.

A second example will help clarify the point that investigating the unconscious is detrimental to therapy. A man who is educated and qualified to practice law fails in his own practice, but does well when he is a subordinate research clerk in a large law firm. Although he says he would like to achieve success, whenever he attempts to strike out on his own he becomes nervous, anxious, and unable to function. Diagnosed as neurotic, he consults a conventional psychiatrist. Eventually he may discover that in his childhood he greatly feared his strong father, a fear accompanied by many fantasies of murdering his father and taking his father's place as the head of the house. These fantasies caused him at that time to fear retaliation, and they still remain in his subconscious mind to produce the conflict between his desire to assert himself and his fear of doing so.

According to traditional theory it is this unconscious conflict which is the obstacle to his getting ahead, since even now he fears to assert himself as a man. Twenty-five years later, whenever he steps from his subordinate, almost childlike role of law clerk, he is unable to function. He is nervous, upset, and ineffective until he retreats from the danger of his independent position to the safety of his clerk's job. According to accepted psychiatric thinking, it is his (now unconscious) childhood conflict, never resolved and continuing throughout his life, which thwarts his success. Maintaining that resolving the conflict is the crux of therapy, the conventional therapist works in the man's past, delving into his unconscious through dreams and free associations in the hope that once these conflicts are uncovered the patient will be able to move ahead successfully.

We accept the fact that a very small portion of his problem may be based upon his past, but we believe that most of it is due to his inability to face what he is really doing now. *Because no one lives a life where his needs are always fulfilled, it is impossible not to find a wealth of buried conflicts which, being similar to present difficulties, seem to explain a person's inability to fulfill his needs now.* This kind of unconscious material comes forth readily under the pressures and skills of the conventional psychiatrist. In addition, the patient soon learns that he can gain the psychiatrist's approval by giving him reams of conflict-causing material. Besides psychiatric approval, the patient likes nothing better than to be relieved of the responsibility for his present behavior by his wonderful storehouse of unconscious conflicts derived from his past failures.

Actually, however, what is really below the level of consciousness is what he is doing now. In a sense the patient is aware of his present behavior, but it is only a meager awareness. Incorrectly assuming that the patient is fully conscious of his present behavior, the conventional therapist emphasizes the past; in so doing *he misses the extent to which the patient lacks awareness of what he is doing now*. The Reality Therapist insists that the patient face his present behavior. We go over and over what he is doing now to make him understand that his *present behavior* does not fulfill his needs.

A further important difference between Reality Therapy and conventional psychiatry concerns the place of morality, or to be more specific, the place of right and wrong in the process of therapy. Conventional psychiatry does not directly concern itself with the issue of right and wrong. Rather, it contends that once the patient is able to resolve his conflicts and get over his mental illness, he will be able to behave correctly. We have found that this view is unrealistic. All society is based on morality, and if the important people in the patient's life, especially his therapist, do not discuss whether his behavior is right or wrong, reality cannot be brought home to him. It is unrealistic to ask a delinquent girl why she stole a car, why she is pregnant, why she smokes marijuana, hoping that once she discovers the reasons she will be able to resolve her conflicts and change her behavior. We believe that to stop her unsatisfactory behavior she must fulfill her needs, but that to fulfill her needs she must face the real world around her that includes standards of behavior.

Admittedly, the introduction of morality into psychotherapy may draw criticism from many sources. Some people argue that a great strength of conventional psychiatry is that it does not involve itself with this age-old question. It would be easier for us if we could avoid the issue also, but we cannot. People come to therapy suffering because they behave in ways that do not fulfill their needs, and they ask if their behavior is wrong. Our job is to face this question, confront them with their total behavior, and *get them to judge* the quality of what they are doing. We have found that unless they judge their own behavior, they will not change. We do not claim that we have discovered the key to universal right or that we are experts in ethics. We do believe, however, that to the best of our ability as responsible human beings, we must help our patients arrive at some decision concerning the moral quality of their behavior. To do so, we have found that for the purpose of therapy the following definition seems to be extremely useful. (Whether our definition could stand the test of scholarly debate with the great moral philosophers of the world is questionable, but at least it has provided us with some framework upon which to focus our therapy discussions.)

We believe that almost all behavior which leads to fulfilling our needs within the bounds of reality is right, or good, or moral behavior, according to the following definition: *When a man acts in such a way that he gives and receives love, and feels worthwhile to himself and others, his behavior is right or moral.*

Usually the law is psychiatrically right (according to the above definition) because human beings with human needs have made the law according to their needs. There are, however, isolated cases where psychiatric right derived from the needs is in conflict with legal right. These cases command widespread publicity because such basic issues are involved. In the murder in Belgium a few years ago of a baby deformed by Thalidomide, the jury acquitted the mother even though she admitted she killed the child. They did so because neither the mother's needs nor the child's needs could be fulfilled with the child living. In this unusual case it might be said that the woman did right psychologically but not legally. The jury, however, forced to balance the mother's needs against a strict legal interpretation, decided that even legally she did not do wrong.

When a person is able to fulfill his need to feel worthwhile to himself and others, there is little conflict over whether his behavior is right, but in many instances the needs are in conflict and it is much more difficult to arrive at the correct course of behavior. For example, when a chief of state gives up his position or a potential chief of state reduces his chances for election because of love, who is really to say that he did right or wrong? Both Edward VIII of England and, more recently, Governor Nelson Rockefeller of New York faced a problem in which there is no absolutely responsible course. In a famous historical example, Socrates chose death rather than life with diminished self-respect, even though he had the assurance of love from friends who urged his escape. A more common situation is one in which a man, discovering his son to be guilty of a crime, is torn between reporting his child or losing his own self-respect.

It is possible to think of hundreds of these moral dilemmas, but it must be made clear that responsible people who are caught in a serious conflict of needs rarely consult a psychiatrist. They recognize that it is up to them to decide what to do.

However, the psychiatrist does see hundreds of patients who have some conflict between their needs and would like to use this as an excuse for irresponsible behavior. For example, a man who is unhappily married gives lip service to continuing the marriage for the sake of his children, but he begins to drink heavily and neglect his work. His income falls off, his family suffers, and his self-respect disappears.

No outsider could solve the problem of such a patient's marriage. He must do that alone. But the psychiatrist who helps him to face the cause of his behavior, curtail his drinking, and resume his adult responsibility toward the support of his family can make a real contribution to this man's development. This is Reality Therapy in action. The patient regains his self-respect and is able to make a decision which is in the best interests of everyone concerned.

A Reality Therapist treating a patient is not afraid to pose the question, "Are you doing right or wrong?" or, "Are you taking the responsible course?" In psychiatric treatment, strengthening the patient's recognition that his present behavior is wrong or irresponsible is a powerful motivation toward positive change. When we point out what the patient is doing which may be wrong instead of helping him look for excuses, he finds out that therapy is not an intellectual psychiatric game of conflict, conflict, what can be the conflict? He discovers that we really care about him, an essential step toward gaining the involvement necessary for therapy.

Therefore, in order to do therapy successfully, the therapist must acknowledge that standards of behavior exist, standards accepted by both individuals and society as the best means of meeting basic human needs. Patients must be confronted by the disparity between the values they recognize as the acceptable norm and the lives they lead.

For example, many delinquent girls maintain that there is nothing wrong with prostitution. Rather than argue, I ask if they would help their daughters become prostitutes. They always answer, "No," but in the next breath they protest that prostitution is the only way they can earn a living—it's all they know.

Getting a patient to acknowledge the values she really believes in is part of the art of therapy, but once acknowledged the major task is to help her live by these standards. Unfortunately, in their effort to avoid the issue of morality, many conventional therapists accept behavior that does not lead to need fulfillment in the mistaken belief that this is the best effort the patient is capable of making.

Where standards and values are not stressed, the most that therapy can accomplish is to help patients become more comfortable in their irresponsibility. Because our effort is always directed toward helping patients fulfill their needs, we insist on their striving to reach the highest possible standards.

We are looking for neither conformity nor mediocrity in the guise of normal behavior. The most responsible men, such as Lincoln or Schweitzer, are those farthest from the norm. Our job is not to lessen the pain of irresponsible actions, but to increase the patient's strength so that he can bear the necessary pain of a full life as well as enjoy the rewards of a deeply responsible existence.

Because the needs can be fulfilled by many different courses of action, reasonable men can have serious conflicts concerning values. An excellent example is the recent controversy over non-denominational prayers in public schools. Some responsible men feel worthwhile without any religion, others without publicly acknowledging religion, and still others do not feel worthwhile unless religion is a part of all life, public and private. Clarence Darrow, Thomas Jefferson, and William Jennings Bryan were living examples of these three categories, in the order stated. Although the resolution of this controversy and similar ones is not within the realm of psychiatry, from the standpoint of Reality Therapy we say that whichever side a person takes, he must examine the reality of what he is doing in all its implications and then decide, as a judge must, what he believes is the correct course.

The final major difference between Reality Therapy and conventional therapy is our emphasis upon the therapist's role as a teacher. In conventional therapy teaching is limited to helping the patient gain insight into the causes of his behavior. From then on it is assumed that he will either learn better ways himself or from someone else; the therapist's job is limited in making clear the conscious and unconscious determinants of his problems.

In Reality Therapy we do not search for the insights so vital to conventional psychiatry. Instead we take every opportunity to teach patients better ways to fulfill their needs. We spend much time painstakingly examining the patient's daily activity and suggesting better ways for him to behave. We answer the many questions that patients ask and suggest ways to solve problems and approach people. Patients who have not been able to fulfill their needs must learn both how to approach people so that they can become more involved and how to accomplish enough so that they can gain an increased feeling of self-worth. The case of Rob, discussed at the end of the previous chapter, illustrates both these points. He was able to become involved with his stepfather and to succeed in college, partly due to having a better approach pointed out. It should be emphasized that he made these changes himself; I only taught him what I believed would make his task easier.

If, analogous to conventional therapy, which stops with insight, Reality Therapy stopped when we succeeded in getting the patient to face reality, our work would be less effective. As important as confronting reality is, it is only part of therapy. The patient must learn to fulfill his needs in the real world he has learned about, and we must teach him how whenever we can. Once involvement is gained and reality is faced, therapy becomes a special kind of education, a learning to live more effectively, that is better and more quickly achieved if the therapist accepts the role of teacher.

To summarize, we should say that in the six major areas covered, Reality Therapy differs markedly from conventional therapy. Reality Therapy is not another variety of the same approach, but a different way to work with people. The requirements of Reality Therapy—an intense personal involvement, facing reality and rejecting irresponsible behavior, and learning better ways to behave—bear little resemblance to conventional therapy and produce markedly different results, as is shown in the succeeding chapters.

Part II | PRACTICE

Introduction

In the following chapters the practice of Reality Therapy is described in situations where it is now in use. The cases are drawn from the practices of the developers of Reality Therapy, Dr. G. L. Harrington and myself.

Chapters 3 and 4 describe the use of Reality Therapy in institutions for delinquent adolescent girls and for psychotic veterans. In both cases therapy is applied primarily in group sessions. We have found that in these situations, where there are many patients with similar problems, group therapy is extremely effective. Individual therapy is still used (most therapists have had their major training and experience in treating individual patients) but the trend is toward groups because of the large number of patients to be seen, and the limited number of therapists available. Primarily because of training and tradition, individual therapy is the choice of most therapists in public and private out-patient practice. Even here, however, there is an increasing trend toward groups as individual treatment does not seem able to keep up with the demand for therapy.

Although in group therapy the therapist may become less involved with each member of the group than he would in individual treatment, this slight loss is more than compensated for by the patients becoming involved with others in the group. Because there is so much more opportunity for involvement, therapy tends to move along more rapidly than usually occurs with the same patients in individual treatment. Patients in similar situations quickly confront each other with reality and are not hesitant to suggest better ways to cope with it. The therapist guides the group toward increasing involvement, intervenes when the group strays from reality, and suggests better ways to cope with reality when the group becomes bogged down. Although he may intervene very little, he remains the leader, usually deciding how long patients are to be kept in a mental hospital or making strong recommendations for length of stay in correctional institutions. Group discussion of the therapist's decisions becomes an important part of the group process and helps the members focus on the important role the therapist plays in their real world.

In contrast to individual treatment, there is a definite time limit for institutional therapy. This is set by the doctor and sometimes, in correctional institutions, by law. Telling patients how long they have in the group before they must leave makes therapy more effective because patients respond to the confidence shown in their ability to become more responsible in a limited time. We are now beginning to apply some treatment time limits to selected private patients with surprisingly good results.

Before turning to the application of Reality Therapy, I must stress again that although the problems described in the next four chapters seem to be different, they are basically the same. The only difference is the way that the patients have chosen to manifest their inability to fulfill their needs. A delinquent who has stolen car after car is no different from the man who suddenly loses all touch with reality and begins directing traffic in a busy street. Both are trying (albeit one more suddenly and seemingly more irrationally than the other) to fulfill their basic needs. Both need to learn better ways to behave, one to learn that he must obey the law if he is to satisfy his needs, the other (attempting dramatically to attract someone's attention to his plight) perhaps to learn to function better in his college studies.

At the moment he steals a car, the auto thief may be more aware of what he is doing than the traffic director, but eventually both will need to face reality by becoming involved with someone through whom they can better fulfill their needs. Neither can excuse his behavior on any ground if he desires help. When each man learns to be more responsible, his particular variety of irresponsible behavior will disappear; therefore, from the standpoint of therapy, what seems so different on the surface is only a variation of the same basic problem. The following four chapters will amply clarify this important point.

3 | The Treatment of Seriously Delinquent Adolescent Girls

THE VENTURA SCHOOL FOR GIRLS

In 1962, on a beautiful level site near Ventura, in the Santa Clara Valley, the state of California opened a new institution for the treatment of older adolescent girls. The previous institution, built between 1914 and 1916, was outdated, overcrowded, and inadequate to house the increasing number of fourteen to twenty-one-year-old girls who were being committed for offenses ranging from incorrigibility to first-degree murder. The low, rambling, one-story red brick buildings, surrounded by a high fence and secure against escape, house approximately four hundred girls from all over California, with the majority from Southern California. A girl committed by the county to the state for transfer to the Ventura School has usually had several years of supervision by county probation services without success. Many have had psychotherapy as a condition of probation; all have been in juvenile halls, some for many months. Profiting little from this treatment, they have continued to break the law. Finally sent to the Ventura School, the last stop before adult prison, they are confined, in most cases, for six to eight months for rehabilitation.

For the most part these girls are very sophisticated, at least in their own milieu. They enter the school often poorly motivated to change toward leading a more responsible life. Usually they have failed in public school through poor attendance and effort; many are poor readers, and few have held any regular job. They are characterized by their lack of deep feeling for themselves or anyone else and by their common history of usually taking to be what they thought the easy, irresponsible course when any choice was presented. Most have multiple self-inflicted tattoos on their arms, legs, and even their faces, a pathetic effort to gain attention from their peers. Initially resentful at being locked up in the security of our institution, few admit that strict custody is probably what they most need.

The job of the school is difficult. Our goal is to take every girl, no matter how antagonistic she may be, and within six to eight months rehabilitate her so that, with the guidance of a parole officer, she will be able to stay out of further serious trouble in the community. Naturally, we do not succeed with everyone, but we do with about 80 per cent of the girls. Operating essentially with an indeterminate commitment, we have permission to keep the seriously irresponsible girls longer if we feel it is necessary; only a few, however, are kept over one year. Although girls who commit serious crimes such as murder, assault with a deadly weapon, or armed robbery are held at the school for one year, these commitments can be reduced if they show signs of earlier rehabilitation. According to our present superintendent, who used to supervise a parole office, 90 per cent of the girls who violate their parole are returned to the institution. Considering that on a recent count out of a total of 370 girls only 43 were returnees, we feel that our program is generally successful.

Since the total program for all girls includes both custody and parole, the return of a girl to the institution is not necessarily an indictment of our efforts. Our job is to continue to work with the girl so that, when she leaves again, she will be able to handle her responsibilities better. As often as possible the parole officer is given definite recommendations for the best way to handle the girl. Skillful parole officers help many girls stay out of further trouble. It is important that I do not give the impression that the school does the whole job. A dedicated parole officer is necessary to continue guiding the girl toward a successful life in the community.

The school program consists of three main parts:

1. *The Custody Program* is administered by warm and skillful counselors who use the principles of Reality Therapy. The girl's knowledge that she is in an institution from which she cannot escape is basic to the program. With the guidance of the staff, she is forced to take the responsibility for her behavior in a total situation where responsibility is continually stressed.

2. *The Treatment Program* is administered by a group of competent psychologists, social workers, and a consulting psychiatrist. The treatment personnel not only work with the girls directly, but they continually work with the custody staff to help them treat the girls according to the principles of Reality Therapy.

3. *The School Program* consists of both academic and vocational courses taught by qualified teachers. All girls have a full daily schedule taking either an academic or a vocational course, or sometimes both. Those who enter the Ventura School with sufficient credits and who stay long enough and complete enough work to graduate receive a regular graduation certificate which does not indicate that it comes from a correctional institution.

Vocational training is given in power sewing; cosmetology; cooking; laundry operation as well as in the specific jobs of waitress, dental assistant, and nurses' aide. Business courses, clerical practice, and business machine operation are also a part of an expanding business program closely attached to the academic classes. The full recreational program includes competitive sports, swimming, and roller skating. Cottage activities include parties, arts and crafts, and housekeeping. Cleanliness and preparation for the tasks that women fulfill are emphasized throughout the program.

All three parts of the program—custody, treatment, and school—work smoothly together so that during her stay the girl experiences a total treatment program in which everyone is interested in her progress. Now she is not allowed to indulge in the irresponsible behavior that she has shown elsewhere. One part of the program is never considered more important than another. For example, no one arrives at the school specifically for psychiatric treatment to the detriment of the rest of the program. Everything we do makes up a treatment program in which the girl is asked from beginning to end to take increasing responsibility. We try to the best of our ability never to allow a girl to leave the school who has not gained in responsibility or who, within our power to predict, cannot live satisfactorily in the community. Naturally we make mistakes, but we have long since stopped releasing girls into the community because we cannot help them or because they do not seem to adjust to the institution. Unless a girl has gained by her stay in the institution, she is not discharged to parole.

The principles of Reality Therapy, as explained in Part I, are applied totally at Ventura School. The superintendent, the psychiatrist, the psychological treatment staff, and the custody counselors all believe that applying these concepts is vital for successful treatment. No one doubts that the problem we are dealing with at Ventura is irresponsibility, that we must get sufficiently involved with the girls so that they wish to become more responsible, and that we must concurrently provide them with a program in which they can demonstrate their progress.

We firmly believe that an institutional training school, or a mental hospital, can produce better results when warm relationships *along with increasing responsibilities* are stressed by an undivided staff. The girl who comes to Ventura has spent her life excusing her behavior in a world where people were not consistent, where one person told her one thing, someone else told her another, and most told her different things from day to day. Every effort must be maintained to provide a unified philosophy of treatment where the staff provides both consistent discipline and warmth and affection. But warmth never supersedes discipline, nor discipline warmth.

INSTITUTIONAL PHILOSOPHY

The philosophy which underlies all treatment at the Ventura School is that mental illness does not exist.

We accept no excuses for irresponsible acts. Students are held responsible for their behavior and cannot escape responsibility on the plea of being emotionally upset, mistreated by mother, neglected by father, or discriminated against by society. Most girls soon learn that the Ventura School is different from any place they have been before. The difference is our caring enough to keep them until they are responsible enough to leave. When they tell us how unfortunate they have been, we accept this uncritically; but from the beginning, in a warm and firm manner, we tell them that while they are here they are responsible for what they do, regardless of how miserable, inconsistent, or unloving the past may have been.

The students learn immediately that we are not interested in their history beyond one important fact: they have broken the law or they would not be in the school. Finding out how bad the past was does not help unless the person can learn better and more responsible ways to behave now and in the future. The girls must learn what responsibility is and act reasonably upon that knowledge. We are interested in what they can do now that will help them live better in the future, such as how they can get along better with their parents, rather than dwelling upon how their parents have treated them in the past.

We are interested in the present, what the student is, and what she must become to be a better person. Each girl learns that we hold her responsible for her behavior, and that we will not send her ill prepared into the world where she must be even more responsible because she will have far less supervision. No policeman will ask why a girl took narcotic drugs. No teacher or principal has the time to investigate in detail why a girl does not come to school; she will simply be excluded if she does not attend. We confront each girl with the reality of the world as it is and point out that, regardless of the difficulties and circumstances, it is up to her to be responsible now. Showing reality to her, however, would be worthless unless we provided a program in which she could learn to be more responsible and demonstrate her progress to her own satisfaction.

In the program we have developed, the student gets a definite school schedule a week after her arrival and is permanently assigned to a cottage. At Ventura status is gained by cooperating with the program, not by defying it. A high standard of performance is expected in the various work and vocational programs, and if the student is in psychiatric treatment, even better behavior is required. Psychiatric treatment is not considered anything more than a part of the program suited to certain girls; it never relieves them of any responsibility. Throughout her stay at the school, each girl is continually evaluated by the staff and she is informed of our evaluation both in person and in writing. We expect her to act better, look better, talk better, and to maintain the school's high standards.

We have discovered that unless we have high standards, the students conclude that we are "phony" and don't really care for them. However, once they are aware of the high standards we maintain by enforcing strict, consistent rules, they realize, perhaps for the first time in their lives, that real care is implied by discipline. We reward them when they accept responsibility and explain that they are not yet ready to go further in the program when they do not accept responsibility. In the latter case, the only major punishment is exclusion from the regular program. The girls are locked in a special cottage, with an in-cottage program which excludes them from the regular school and from their own cottage. When they show enough responsibility, they are allowed to leave this cottage and return to the school program. Confinement is not held against them, although of course they lose time from the regular program. Only by strictly enforcing understandable rules can we teach the girls that we mean what we say, and that they must take the responsibility for their behavior.

Our school program, therefore, must be attractive enough so that exclusion from it is indeed painful. In addition, it is up to the institution to work toward developing an increasingly better program—one that is more interesting, more effective, and more mature. The students must feel that we are never satisfied with the status quo, but that we are continually trying to provide them with every opportunity to better themselves and to find some happiness when they do so. Unlike punishment, removal from the program is a positive measure, a motivation for the girls to work hard to return to a program in which they learn that responsibility is not an abstract word but a vital experience.

THE GIRLS

A school for older delinquent girls is thought to be a prisonlike institution housing droves of antagonistic, hard-boiled, tough-talking, sex-starved girls who are intensely resistant to reforming their ways.Those who work there are imagined to be tough, wisecracking, hostile, and cleverly suspicious of everything the girls do, especially of any good behavior. These common movie, TV, or popular magazine stereotypes are actually completely false. Ventura may house the most delinquent adolescent girls in California, but a visitor to the school is hard pressed to recognize them as such. He sees a group of girls, laughing, talking, and moving freely around the school with seemingly little supervision or restraint. They appear little different from a group of girls in a high school in a middle-class neighborhood except that they are a little plumper (institution food is high in calories) and not too well dressed (girls artificially separated from boys tend to let their dress go, as much as we encourage them not to).

The girls are friendly and outgoing and, to a visitor's surprise, they talk with pride about "their" school. There is a decided absence of toughness, sexiness, and hostility so that a casual observer wonders why these girls are locked up or where the really tough girls are hidden. He also notes the absence of any racial tension, seeing white, Negro, and Mexican-American girls mixing with obvious warmth and friendship.

The counselors and teachers appear little different from the staff at any local high school. An experienced observer ordinarily cannot detect any attitude or behavior in the staff which leads him to believe that the girls are greatly different from ordinary teenagers.

The visitor's impression of both girls and staff is not completely accurate. We do have tough girls, hostile girls, and antagonistic girls, but they do not stand out because our program is set up to help them control the kind of behavior which got them into trouble. Out of the almost four hundred girls at Ventura, there are usually one or two kept in the discipline cottage because their behavior is too disruptive to allow them to mix with the other girls. They may stay months in this cottage while they are worked with intensively to help them learn control. The remaining ten to fifteen girls in the discipline cottage are not long-term, serious problems, but they have broken various rules. They will stay from two days to two weeks in close custody in a program in which they can demonstrate through their attitude and cooperation that they are ready to go back to their regular cottage on campus. In the warm, firm custody of Ventura the girls quickly learn the benefits of conforming to sensible rules. Controlling their behavior is a new experience for most of the girls and, despite occasional griping, they are happy to do so because for many their stay at Ventura is the first time they have fulfilled their needs. An atmosphere in which the girls live in a good relationship to the staff (and in which many of them admit they are genuinely happy) is a necessary requisite for any girl to start to change. In many cases in which the irresponsibility is not too extensive, the regular program is sufficient to cause change.

The environment at Ventura, which derives from the principles of Reality Therapy, has not just happened. The result of great effort and good planning, it takes constant vigilance to maintain. As quickly as we can, we strive to get humanly involved with each girl. Most often it is one or more of the cottage staff who break through, sometimes a school teacher, very often a therapist, and sometimes a member of the administrative staff, including the superintendent.

Recently we have innovated a volunteer program in which interested women from the surrounding community visit a girl who has no family or regular visitors. When she is ready, they take her off grounds, treating her as if they were her family. We found that some girls without families who have been in foster homes and institutions for years before coming to Ventura rejected our best efforts because we were part of the institution world in which the girl had been so miserable. She would not give us a chance to show her we might be different because she had so little hope. However, a volunteer who is not part of our institution, who can generously show affection for the girl, can often begin an involvement through which we can reach her further.

As an aid to the reader in understanding our girls and their problems, let me introduce some girls whom I have treated over the years. I have selected these girls because each presented a special problem which led us to believe that we would have to make an extra effort to reach them and help them to improve their behavior. We of the therapy staff may add to the whole school program that extra human touch necessary to reach these girls.

JERI

Jeri was referred to me because the record stated that she was potentially suicidal. She was in the discipline cottage, not because she had broken rules, but because she had said that she would not go out into the school program. If we did not put her in a room and leave her alone, she said she would try to kill herself. In the discipline unit, she cried a great deal, alternating the crying with periods of hysterical laughter. She was intent on creating the impression that she belonged in a mental hospital instead of Ventura. A psychiatrist is usually asked to see girls like Jeri because the staff feels uncomfortable without some special guidance. About a week before, I had seen her briefly for an initial interview during which she said that she wanted no part of the school and would not cooperate in the program. Having heard this many times before from girls who had just arrived, I did not take it seriously. Evidently she had meant what she said, for she had succeeded in getting herself removed from the program and in worrying the staff about her sanity.

Jeri was a short, attractive, intelligent sixteen-year-old girl who had caused so much conflict in her home in Florida that her parents had sent her to an uncle in San Francisco. Shortly after arriving in San Francisco, she ran away from her uncle and, for the eighteen months before coming to Ventura, had supported herself in the San Francisco area by shoplifting. Living with a group of older girls and women who stole for their support, she was involved in criminal activities as much as any of her older companions or even more than they. She posed as nineteen, refused to admit her true age, and boasted that at least one large department store in San Francisco must be out of the red now that she was locked up. Many of the things she stole she had no use for; much was wasted, thrown away, or given away. The act of stealing expensive furs, for example, was more important than the furs themselves.

Jeri was committed to the California Youth Authority because she was caught stealing an inexpensive blouse from a Southern California store on an infrequent trip south. She complained bitterly that she should have just been put in jail for ten days as an adult instead of having to go to the California Youth Authority. It was like slipping on a banana peel after successfully shooting Niagara Falls.

In our initial conversation I said I wanted to help her get out of Ventura and stay out of trouble, but I could not do anything for her unless she would consent to leave her room in the discipline cottage. Although agreeing that she was upset, I told her I believed she felt upset mainly because she had been caught. I refused to discuss her threat of suicide, and when she brought it up I told her what I usually tell girls who threaten to take their lives, "We can't help you if you kill yourself. We have no program for girls who threaten suicide, and there is absolutely no chance of your being transferred to a mental hospital."[1] Adding that she was welcome to spend as much time as she wished in her room in the discipline cottage, I noted that the time spent there would be of no use in helping her. I repeated I would like to help her, that we had a good program, and that we wanted her to give it a chance. This part of the conversation was blended into a friendly get-acquainted discussion of our school, our program, of me and my work, and of her life over the past few months. Although I did not agree with her method, I did respect her attempt to assert herself, and I intimated that the same effort in a different direction might do her much more good.

When I left, we were on good terms. She promised nothing and I did not push her for a decision about leaving the discipline cottage. I told her, however, that this was the last time I would see her there although I would be happy to see her in my office if she changed her mind. Altogether it was a pleasant interview in which I was completely honest and serious with her. I wrote a note telling the staff to pay no attention to her desire to be recognized as mentally ill, not to worry that she would commit suicide, and to leave her alone to think over what I had said.

Three days later when I came back to the school there was a note from Jeri saying that she had decided "to give up acting

[1] Very few girls are transferred to mental hospitals because generally we have much better facilities for treating girls with any kind of irresponsibility, including psychosis.

crazy," that she had entered the school program, and that she wanted to see me in my office. When she came she made light of what she had done in the discipline cottage and put on a determined effort to be friendly and ingratiating. Saying she had come into the program as a favor to me, she wanted to know how soon I was going to get her out. I said that when she was released depended upon how she acted in the program, adding that I would be glad to see her regularly once a week for half an hour. Because at that time I did not have a group to place her in and because I had not seen a patient individually for a long while, I decided to do so for a change, although it is not my regular practice at Ventura.

At best, she behaved only adequately in the program. Our conversations were mostly friendly arguments in which she concentrated on what I could do for her and how "we" would work to get her out. Telling her that it was up to her and not me, I tried with little success to break through her shell to find some interest. Instead, she discussed how she would go back to stealing.

All during therapy and especially toward the time that she would ordinarily have been considered ready for parole, I pointed out to her that she had little feeling for anyone in the world except herself. I told her that as much as I enjoyed talking to her and as well as she seemed to be doing at times in the kitchen program, unless she began to consider the rights and feelings of other people, both here at the school and in the community, she would go right back to being a thief when she left. I always emphasized the word *thief,* never glossing over the offense with the milder euphemism, shoplifter. At the same time I heard that in the cottage she did everything possible to avoid work while still looking as if she was busy.

When the time came for referral to parole, the big moment at Ventura, the housemother did not think that she had sincerely tried to work into the program, and she was especially influenced to refuse to recommend her when Jeri said, "You have to refer me because Dr. Glasser thinks I'm doing good." I had already told the housemother to hold her if she did not feel she was ready, and Jeri was really shaken when her time at the school was extended a month. She threatened to go back to her old "crazy" behavior. She cried, she disparaged her housemother, she claimed I broke my promises, said I had no real influence, and that the school was unfair.

During the next month she did not do well. As much as she complained of my inadequacy to my face, she began to spread rumors that she was "in" with me, and that I would do anything for her. Part of this behavior is natural for a girl who is getting involved with a person who has some status, a kind of name-dropping, but when it continues as it did here, it becomes a way for her to escape from responsibility. It was necessary to confront her with what she was doing. The climax came after I warned her several times about saying that I was doing favors for her. Despite her bland denials, I heard from several sources, staff and other girls, that she had said I had mailed letters for her, a serious violation of our strict rule about censoring mail.

When I definitely confirmed that she had said it, I went to her cottage and told her that she would have to go to the discipline unit. As difficult as it is to confront and discipline a girl who is in therapy, I had no choice. Knowing how uncomfortable it made me, she played my discomfort for all it was worth. She put on an emotional scene in front of all the girls in the cottage, stating that my charges were all lies, that I only wanted to lock her up to keep her from leaving, that my attempt to help her was phony, and that she never wanted to see me again. I listened, restated that I wanted to help her, and told her I would see her next at our regular time in the discipline cottage. She walked away crying and saying that I could not be her friend or help her any more. She made it sound as if I had committed the unpardonable sin by confronting her with the reality of her behavior. Actually, she was testing my intentions, trying to find out whether I really did care what she did and what she said, whether I could stand up to her attempt to downgrade me in front of the other girls, and whether I would show retaliatory anger. Girls are willing to accept discipline but not punishment; they differentiate between the two by seeing whether the disciplining person shows anger and gets satisfaction by exercising power. What followed worked only because I neither felt nor showed that I was punishing her.

The following week when I went to the discipline unit Jeri was anxious to see me. As soon as she came into the office it was apparent that our involvement had been strengthened. My standing firm and rejecting her irresponsible behavior without rejecting her, as evidenced by my continued interest in seeing her after all that she had said about me, had broken through.

She was greatly changed. She asked me how long she would have to stay in the discipline cottage. Saying that I would leave it up to her to tell me when she was ready to leave, I helped her by adding that she could prepare for leaving by telling the truth and changing some of her ways. She then poured out the story of her deceitful life, her lies and misbehavior at the school, and how worried she was about her future. Instead of forgiving her, which used to be my natural impulse before I discovered how wrong it is therapeutically, I told her she was right to feel miserable and probably would continue to feel bad for the next few weeks. When I left I told her I would see her next week. Her desire to stay in discipline was therapeutic—knowing that she had thinking to do and feelings of guilt to overcome, she realized that the discipline cottage was the best place for her.

In Reality Therapy it is important not to minimize guilt when it is deserved, and Jeri deserved to feel as bad as she did. Although she felt better the next week, she still did not think she was ready to leave the discipline unit. We talked mostly of her future and how she would have to take care of herself. Not wanting to go back to Florida to her family, she requested that she be paroled to a foster home in San Diego, which we arranged. The following week, after three weeks in discipline, she was ready to return to her cottage. The remainder of the time in therapy was spent planning in detail what she would do when she was released, especially how she would avoid old friends and old temptations. She left after eight months, three and a half months more than our minimum program. Everyone noticed how much she had changed, particularly her housemother, whom she now loved—a great contrast with earlier times when she had told me how hateful and prejudiced her housemother was.

In summary, we could see that when Jeri tested me to find out whether I really cared, there was enough involvement for me to pass the test in her eyes by placing her in discipline. If I had not done so she would never have changed; if we had not been moderately involved it would not have worked. When I rejected her irresponsibility but maintained interest in her, our involvement solidified, and she then began to fulfill her needs. The rest of therapy was relearning, mainly detailed planning for her future.

MARIA

Apathetic and despondent, Maria, a seventeen-and-a-half-year-old girl, was a far different problem from Jeri. Jeri was at least capable of taking care of herself fairly well, albeit illegally. She had good intelligence and some sort of warped self-reliance. Maria, on the other hand, had almost nothing. In institutions since she was about twelve, before then in foster homes, with no family, few friends, not too much intelligence (although test results are misleadingly low on these deprived girls), she came to my attention after she was involved in a serious fight in her cottage. I was asked to see her in the discipline cottage because she seemed so hopeless. She had been sitting in her room, eating little, and making no effort to contact any of the cottage staff. There seemed to be little we could do for her because she had given up herself. The fight that brought her into discipline was the result of a building frustration caused by an older, smarter girl, Sonia, who, recognizing Maria's desperate need for affection, pretended to like her in order to get Maria to be a virtual slave. Maria had attacked another girl whom Sonia had openly preferred to her and who joined with Sonia in making fun of Maria.

When I sat with her in the day room of the discipline unit, she refused to speak, just sitting apathetically and staring at the floor. I asked her my routine getting-acquainted questions, such as, How long have you been at the school? What are you here for? What are your plans? Do you want to return to your cottage? Maria just sat and stared. Finally she asked me to leave her alone. She had seen plenty of psyches (as our girls call psychiatrists) before, but she never talked to them. It was a discouraging interview, if it could be called an interview at all. We were worlds apart. After about twenty very long minutes I said, "I will see you next week." Saying nothing, she walked quietly back to her room. I felt that I had made no impression whatsoever. None!

Each week for seven weeks the same scene was repeated, except for different questions, and few enough of them because I could not think of what to ask. My most frequent question was, "Don't you want to get out of here?" Her reply, on occasions when she did reply, was, "What for?" My attempts to answer were met with silence. I did not have a good answer because she was obviously involved with no one and had no way to fulfill her needs—her isolated room was probably the most comfortable place for her. At least in a room by herself she did not have to see others doing and feeling what was not possible for her.

At the eighth visit I detected the first glimmer of hope. She said "Hi" in answer to my "Hi" and looked at me occasionally during the interview. I decided on a whim to ask her about her tattoos. Tattoos are the rule with our girls; nine girls out of ten have some. On her legs and arms Maria had twenty or thirty self-inflicted tattoos —dots, crosses, words, initials, and various marks, all common with our girls. I asked her if she would like a large, particularly ugly tattoo removed. Unexpectedly, she said she would; she would like them all out. Her request surprised me because girls like Maria are more apt to add tattoos rather than want them out. Lonely, isolated girls, particularly in juvenile halls, derive some sense of existence through the pain of pushing ink or dirt into their skin and by the mark produced by the act. It is a way they have, they tell me, of making sure they are still there. On the next visit we talked further about her tattoos and her feelings of hopelessness. In addition, she brought up her fear that her housemother, toward whom she had some warm feeling, would not take her back into the cottage because of what she had done. Although a housemother can refuse to take a girl back into the cottage when there are serious fights between girls, she rarely does so. I said I did not know whether or not her housemother would take her back, but that I could have her housemother stop by and see her if Maria wished it. She said she would appreciate seeing her housemother very much.

Maria now started to make progress. Her housemother, who liked her and recognized the loneliness in her quiet, uncomplaining ways, visited her and told her she was welcome back in the cottage. Her housemother also said how much she missed Maria's help with the cottage housework. Maria had been a tireless worker in the cottage. I told Maria that I had discussed her problems with the girls in my therapy group and that they wanted her to join the group. My few interviews, together with the powerful effect of the housemother's visit, had already caused some change in Maria when she left discipline. The girls in my group therapy took a special interest in her, something which might have been resented by a more sophisticated girl, but was deeply appreciated by Maria. The technique of getting girls who are more responsible to become particularly interested in someone like Maria is strongly therapeutic for them because it directly leads to fulfilling their needs and helps them to identify with the staff, thereby helping to sever ties with their own delinquent group.

Taking more interest in school, Maria began to learn to read for the first time. In the group we talked at length about what she might do, and it was decided that a work home with small children, whom she could love and who might love her in return, would be best. Older girls who have no families do well in carefully selected homes where they are paid to do housework and child care. Although by then she was no problem, we kept her a few extra months so that some of her worst tattoos could be removed and to allow her to become more accustomed to relating to people.

The case of Maria illustrates that the key to involvement is neither to give up nor to push too hard. No matter how lonely and isolated a girl may be, if the therapist adheres to the present and points to a hopeful future and, in cases like Maria's, expands her initial involvement into a series of involvements as soon as possible, great changes can take place. Here the need for group therapy was critical for there she could gain strength from relating to more responsible girls and could see how she might emulate their more responsible behavior. Through our persistence Maria, perhaps for the first time in her life, was able to fulfill her needs.

From her good relationship with her housemother, Maria was able to go to a work home where her hard work and love for children were deeply appreciated. Later she married and our asssistant superintendent has several pictures of Maria's growing and successful family in her "grandchildren" picture gallery.

TERRY AND LIZ

Not all the girls I am called to see spend time in the discipline cottage although many do. Two who did not were Terry and Liz, who came to the school at about the same time from a county institution where they had seriously broken the rules. Terry had been in custody on and off for four years before she arrived at Ventura. She had been incorrigible in previous institutions, and the last one gave up on her when she got drunk on a long-planned-for day at home.

Sent to us as the last resort, she was a pretty but extremely tense sixteen-year-old who, when I first saw her, demanded that I do something to make her less nervous. She evidently had been taking a variety of different tranquilizer drugs at the previous institution, and even before I took her into therapy she cornered me in her cottage where I was eating lunch and demanded medication for her nerves. With the demand she gave me a lecture on the varieties and activities of tranquilizer drugs that would have been a model for a pharmacologist. I refused, explaining that no tranquilizers of any kind were used at Ventura because I did not believe they helped the girls. Tranquilizers help people escape from facing reality; they should only be given to people who are in good control or to those who are so far out of control that they need physical restraints, such as a violent patient in a mental hospital who may need cuffs. We have neither type of girl at Ventura. I told her that I was the only person who could prescribe tranquilizers so that throwing a tantrum for someone else would not help. I explained that if she thought acting upset would get me to prescribe tranquilizers, now was her chance. She could throw her best tantrum and I would be glad to sit with her and we would discuss it, but there was nothing in terms of bad behavior that I hadn't seen a thousand times previously and I had long since given up prescribing drugs for temper outbursts.

My remarks surprised her greatly. Previously, professional people had responded to her nervousness and threats of acting out by unwittingly, but from her viewpoint solicitously, relieving her of the responsibility for her behavior with large doses of tranquilizer drugs. As she continued to threaten to break windows and to fall apart from nervous tension, I told her something that I believe started our involvement.

"Terry," I said, "Ventura is different from any other place you have been. Here you have the right to suffer, and we will respect your suffering. You probably have good reason to feel bad, but you will not learn anything if we give you pills. In fact, I'm sure that the more pills you received in the last institution, the more you misbehaved and then blamed it on the pills. You do the same thing yourself with liquor and reds and yellows [illegally obtained seconal and nembutal] when you are home, but you won't be allowed to here." Adding that I would welcome her into my group therapy where I would help her find better ways to behave so that she could feel better, I emphasized that at Ventura we believe that what you do, more than what you feel, is important. I am not beyond explaining Reality Therapy, in a sense, to the girls because they understand, more than most of us, the truth in stressing behavior over feelings. She agreed, as have countless other girls, that the pills increase their acting out by giving them an excuse for it (they say the pills make them goofy so they can't control themselves), and she never asked for them again.

Terry came into group and did well. In the beginning she tested me continually by asking for favors and by threatening me with bad behavior; each time, when I did not give in, we became more involved. Her acting out stopped and she began to be helpful in the cottage. Noticing her change toward maturity, her housemother gave her more responsibility. Terry often remarked that she could not believe it herself when she found herself working and acting decently; she had never done anything before but create havoc. As much as Terry improved in Ventura, we found that planning her future was difficult. She had been in institutions so long that we did not feel she would be able to adjust to the relatively free atmosphere which she would find in public school. She was too young to work and she could count on little from her parents, who were estranged from her both by the years of custody and by her previous behavior. Their attitude was, "Let the state care for her," and this atmosphere where the burden of proof was on Terry was too much. She is an example of a girl who needs a halfway house where she can enter the community and still have the security of a good place to live, staffed by interested people who can direct or supervise her progress. We felt that as she gradually learned to cope with freedom and show this knowledge to her parents, she might then slowly and carefully return home.

After five months on parole, much longer than she had been able to stay out previously, she ran away from home with a boyfriend, hoping to get married. They stole a car in the process and she is now writing me from a jail in Oklahoma. Even this behavior was not all bad; it was her attempt to prove she is a woman because she had believed for many years that she was homosexual. Her success in relating to me and to male teachers at Ventura had helped her feel female, but unfortunately we released her too soon into a world too difficult for her to handle.

As much as we try not to release girls before they are ready, sometimes we make mistakes. When Terry returns to Ventura, as she writes she hopes she will, I think we can help her stay out of further trouble. Desperately lonely when she came to Ventura, she has started to learn to fulfill her needs. Besides an attempt to establish her sexual identity, her runaway may have been her way of returning for more help; even though Ventura is therapeutic, you have to break the law to get in. With a poor home situation, she was not yet strong enough to find someone responsible outside her home. Terry represents a girl who will have to make at least two trips through the school, as about 15 to 20 per cent of our girls do. Hopefully, each time something is gained as we continue to apply Reality Therapy, building from where we were when the girl left.

After Terry had been in the group awhile, she asked if her "sister" Liz, who had by then arrived, could join. Although their sisterhood was the result of an "adoption" (by Terry) at a previous institution, they did have a striking physical resemblance. Often it is good to allow girls who are old friends to be in the same group even when it is obvious that initially they want to be together just to have more time to talk to each other, especially if they are not in the same cottage. We do not mind being manipulated a little because, after we point out what is happening, they push each other toward more responsibility.

When Liz joined the group, the two girls had a big reunion to impress everyone. Although they immediately started talking over their delinquent activities of the past, Liz was surprised that Terry had settled down so well. She was especially surprised that Terry was not in the discipline cottage because she had lived in the discipline unit for almost two years in the previous institution.

Liz was quite different from Terry. Coming from a good home, she had therefore spent much less time in custody. Her activities included many runaways, sexual delinquency, barbiturate and benzedrine pills, and some gang associations. From the record one would expect her to be more hostile, but she was just the opposite, as smooth and sweet as a girl could be. It was hard to imagine her participating in a small riot, for which she had been removed from the previous institution. Expecting to be sent home after the riot as an institutional failure (an example of how unrealistically some of the girls think), she was shocked to be at Ventura.

At Ventura Liz had made up her mind to "snow" us with sweetness in order to leave as soon as possible to return to her own ways. As much as she was devoted to Liz, Terry made it a point to explain Liz's poor attitude to the group. Terry's ability to face reality for Liz is an example of one of the reasons why group therapy works so well. Girls who refuse to admit their own problems easily see the problems of others in facing reality, and they can accept this confrontation more easily from each other than from a therapist. Terry also wanted Liz to change because Liz had a devoted family which Terry hoped she might eventually join. In contrast to Terry, whose rather nondescript family of four children included at that time one brother in the California Youth Authority, another in jail, and a two-and-a-half-year-old sister at home, Liz was the only one in trouble in a rather stable, upper middle-class family. Terry begged me to allow her to go home with Liz, which would not have been a bad idea if Liz's mother had been interested. Almost any parole plan that has a chance of working will be considered. Stranger plans than this have been approved and worked well.

To avoid facing reality, Liz tried to be a junior therapist in the group, blandly assuming the role of the perfectly reformed girl who was eager to point out to others the futility of their ways. With my support the group turned the tables on her, forcing her to examine her own behavior despite her efforts to avoid it. We soon recognized that she always blamed everything that happened on others, maintaining the role of the unfortunate victim of circumstances. If I pointed this out to her, she would say that I, too, was against her, and therapy would be stalled. To help her face reality and stop wasting time blaming me, I told her that she could leave when she made at least a C in each of her classes. I knew this requirement would present no problem for her except in her major course, cosmetology, which she was failing because she refused to follow the regular course of instruction. She wanted only to set hair and not do any of the rest of the work. In her usual way she blamed the teacher, bitterly assailing her attitude which, in Liz's words, caused a personality clash. She refused to admit that she ought to learn the whole course as the other girls did. When her grade, which she received each month, continued to be failing, I showed her a note that I wrote to the progress committee saying that I would not recommend that she be paroled unless she raised her cosmetology grade.

As much as she blamed me and the group for agreeing that a C grade was necessary if she wanted to leave, she had to change her know-it-all attitude in cosmetology. All her life she had used her sweet, seemingly congenial disposition to get away with whatever she wanted to do. Frustrated because her regular ways were not working, she did not want to put forth the effort to do anything more than act nice. After several months during which she tried every way to avoid doing better in cosmetology, she finally started to work a little harder. The group pressure, mostly exerted by Terry, started the change in her behavior, which in turn led her to become involved with the group and to recognize that they really cared for her, as shown by their efforts for her.

When she began to change, we started to apply new pressure. Although her grades were now satisfactory and she was ready to leave, we were afraid that she might slip into her old ways when she left. To help prevent her failing, we were able to take advantage of an unusual circumstance. Each Monday her mother visited, bringing loads of unrealistic encouragement along with the goodies to eat. Her mother steadfastly refused to see Liz for what she was and, unless she did, we knew Liz would not change greatly when she got home. I suggested that we include her mother in the group meeting, something I had never done before, and the group readily agreed. With Liz's mother present the group described, as only our girls can when they talk about themselves realistically, the details of what Liz had done and planned to do again at home. Now both Liz and her mother became involved in the group and, to their mutual surprise, much more with each other. With our support, her mother changed from a seemingly helpless, manipulated, guilt-ridden, inadequate woman to someone who now began to play the mother's role with some authority.

In the beginning her mother whined that Liz would only run away again as she had done in the past when she insisted on proper behavior, but the group hammered home to the mother that it was her job to call the parole officer when Liz broke rules. She was told that it would show she did not really love Liz if she did not do so. The group demanded discipline, and Liz began to demand it too. She agreed that perhaps she could be different if her mother would call her bluff. Dropping more and more of her old "you can't really touch me" defenses, for the first time she really began to talk to us. She expressed her fear of rejection in her local high school and admitted that she sought her friends in minority races not because race made no difference to her but because she felt enough superior to them so they would not reject her.

Because her family had moved, Liz could get a new start, but whether she took advantage of the new start was up to her. We stressed the now, the reality, the necessity to learn new ways of better behavior. Although when she left she had begun to realize that there was more in life for her than delinquency, it would have been better if we could have kept her longer at Ventura to gain more strength. She has succeeded on parole because she has so much support, but I am worried about what will happen to her when she is off parole. Although most girls are discharged about two years after release if they stay out of trouble, girls like Liz should be kept on a long parole, perhaps to the limit of the law, until age twenty-one. Sometimes in the same predicament I have asked girls to stay longer, honestly admitting I was mistaken in saying they would be ready to leave, and a few have stayed on. I knew Liz would not, so I did not ask.

What the group and I accomplished in all these cases could only have occurred against the background of our school program. If the program did not complement the efforts of all the individuals on the staff who struggle to reach the girls, we would have little success. It is safe to say that none of these girls would have responded to therapy in an uncontrolled out-patient setting, and they would have changed very little in an institution in which Reality Therapy was not practiced.

SHARON

Wednesday
November 6, 1963

Dear Dr. Glasser,

Hello, hello, hello!—and how are you? I'm better'n ever and hope to hear that you're the same.

Whether you know it or not I've been home almost two months and I hope you haven't forgotten me! But seriously, almost sixty days of my 90 day "danger period" are over, and believe it or not I couldn't be better! I've been doing all the typical teen-age things that are quite normal such as buying clothes, going out, and getting along with my Mother. (Who, incidentally, isn't a "square," (to use your favorite expression) as I thought.) In fact, she's pretty cool.

How is your book coming along? Or have you finished? The last I remember you were trying to figure a way to start the last chapter. You'll have to tell me the name of it again, and once it's published I *promise* to read it.

Come tomorrow I'll have been working a month. You can't beat it. Up at 6:30 A.M. and down by 11:00 P.M.—on week nights, of course, week ends are different but not too much!

My P.O. was here about two and a half weeks ago and she seems o.k. She gave me permission to see Mildred which made me very happy. My Mom volunteered to be with us *etc.* and chaperone us for the first couple months, but as soon as she feels we're fairly immune to temptation she'll let us go places on our own. Like I said, you can't beat it!

I started out to write just a few lines but as usual, I've gone on and on. Anyway, if you'd like to write I'll enjoy hearing from you again.

Best regards,
Sharon

This letter introduces Sharon, a sophisticated and now happy teenager since her stay at Ventura. During my brief routine interview of new arrivals, she impressed me as a girl who would be difficult to reach. She seemed bored with the whole idea of Ventura and thought that psychiatrists were the silliest part of any institutional program. She made it clear to me that she wanted to be left alone and that she did not want any psychiatric treatment, especially the kind we offered. During her stay at the reception center, where new girls are screened, she got a fairly accurate impression of Reality Therapy, including the fact that we held girls responsible for their behavior, and she wanted none of it. It seemed to me, however, that in our first interview, hard as she was working to convince me she did not care, a mutual recognition passed between us. She knew I knew her secret and it made her uncomfortable. By this I mean she knew I knew how lonely she really was. She also felt that I refused to believe that she wanted no one except for what she could get from them, and that I was going to do my best to poke my nose into her business at Ventura. Perhaps even at our first encounter we became a little involved, but there was a long way to go.

Sharon was a beautiful, very intelligent sixteen-year-old girl who had entered college, having graduated from high school early because she had gone to school in custody the year around for the past two and one-half years. She was sent to Ventura for running away from home, failing to report to her probation officer, living illegally with a man, and taking occasional narcotic pills. She was also suspected of homosexuality, prostitution, and petty theft. It was not these offenses that made her such a difficult case, however; it was her refusal to allow anyone to get really close to her.

Because she had already graduated from high school, she was assigned to work rather than to classes at school. Although she worked efficiently as a student secretary in the school office, we began to hear complaints that she was using her position to manipulate girls and, in subtle ways, even staff. She influenced girls to ask for certain classes in which they could be with their friends, promised to intercede with the principal on behalf of the girls, generally acted the big shot, and got girls to do her favors for what she supposedly was doing for them.

During this time I had been seeing her informally at her cottage after lunch. My routine at that time was to eat in her cottage and spend time after lunch talking to the girls, who are free to relax for about forty-five minutes. Although we became friendly in a superficial way, I was still very much the outsider trying to reach her. She responded by toying with my attempts to get close, pretending to be nice, yet underneath laughing at me and what I represented of the Ventura program. She often said, "I'll do whatever you want me to do here, and I will not be back," intimating she would be too smart to be caught again. My response, and this became an old refrain, was, "It doesn't look as if you will be leaving here for a long time; you're not ready." When she asked why I answered, "You will have to figure that out. I really can't tell you, but I will tell you when you are ready to leave."

Believing that I was just making conversation, she enjoyed what she thought was a game until she was passed over when the time came for referral to parole. She was told, "Dr. Glasser did not think you were ready." At our next after-lunch talk she asked, "Did you really hold me up?" She could not believe it. When I answered, "Yes," she did not get angry. Smiling, she said, "That's okay, I like it here; I'll stay." Her whole aim was to make me feel foolish in my attempt to affect her in any way.

We continued to talk as before, mostly about books. Because I had read many of the books she was reading, we were able to have some genuine discussions, but she did little more than acknowledge by her friendly attitude that she enjoyed our talks. Resentment, however, was building inside her, especially as our conversations indicated I was not disturbed by her lack of progress. While she continued to be nice to everyone, she stepped up her campaign to divide the people in the school office and cause trouble, both to get revenge against us and also in the hope we would get tired of her and throw her out. Working very hard, she gained great favor with the academic school principal, who used her as his private secretary. Because she was so intelligent and efficient, he was not immediately aware that she was using her position to lord it over the other students and to snub the regular office staff. Eventually her behavior caused a disturbance in the school office and, because I knew her better than anyone, I was asked to see her.

In my office for the first time, Sharon blandly asked me what all the fuss was about, knowing full well that the school office was in a turmoil because of her. When I confronted her with the facts, she denied everything. Disregarding her denial, I told her that finally we had something to work on. Rather than removing her from the office, I would point out the behavior that we considered wrong, and if she wanted to help herself, she could correct it. Knowing that it would take time for her to improve her behavior, I told her that from now on she had to see me regularly. She said she would not. I told her that she was in serious trouble because of the commotion she had created in the school office, and if she refused to see me to help her change, I would place her in the discipline unit. She looked right at me and said, "You would, wouldn't you?" I replied, "I won't have to. You'll come, won't you?" She said, "I'll think it over." Giving her until Monday (this was Thursday), I told her if she did not come then I would see her next in the discipline unit. She left in a mild huff, but on Monday she came to my office.

It might appear that threatening Sharon would be the worst way to start therapy, because our relationship, tenuous as it was, would be weakened rather than strengthened. Actually she had been looking for someone who was genuinely interested in her and who was tough enough to mean what he said. At the same time she could feel the pain it caused me to have to threaten her. Had the threat been made with any feeling on my part of "now I was going to show her," she probably would still be in discipline, but she understood me correctly even as she did in the interview when she first arrived. What happened here illustrates the crux of therapy. Patients want you to correct their irresponsible behavior, but they want it to be done in the genuine spirit of helping them, not to satisfy yourself by winning a power struggle. This is the caring that leads to involvement. Unless Sharon could feel that I was truly interested in helping her, she would never let down her guard.

When she came to therapy on Monday she did not refer to the past Thursday except to say that she was going to stop causing trouble in the office. At the end of our interview she asked when I was going to recommend her for referral. I told her, "As soon as possible," which means about three months in our program during which time she could demonstrate her sincerity. Answering this question affirmatively so soon after her change of attitude was critical in Sharon's case. She was asking me to trust her change of attitude and I did. She was ready to show us but she needed this trust to start. It takes experience to recognize this point and even with experience we make mistakes, but we did not with Sharon. Because the timing is a necessary part of keeping faith, the indeterminate commitment we have at Ventura is a great advantage. Correctional institutions which have rigid sentence structures are severely handicapped in their rehabilitation efforts.

Now our conversation shifted to her biggest problem, how she was going to live with her mother. As can be seen by the second paragraph of her letter, we succeeded in solving the problem. When she treated her mother well, her mother responded by treating her better. Many of our girls do this and later remark, as did Sharon, "Mother is so changed." Her parole officer, whose recent visit to Ventura was a year after Sharon left the school, could not say enough good things about her. Telling us that she will miss Sharon when she leaves parole, which will be soon, she cannot understand why I was concerned about her. "She is such a pleasure to have in my case load," were her words.

LINDA

Finally, I would like to introduce some letters written by Linda, a girl with whom I worked intensively, but who gave us no trouble at the school despite her stormy course in previous institutions. We became involved following our first impromptu lunch table conversation in the same cottage that Sharon later came to. Her first words, stated with mock seriousness, were: "Dr. Glasser, I'm here because I'm a very emotionally disturbed girl." I answered on the same note, "I can't understand that. Our girls aren't here because they are emotionally disturbed, only because they violated the law. If your only trouble is being emotionally disturbed, I will make it my business to get you out of here because we don't understand anything about complicated psychiatric problems like that." Then I asked her whether, besides being emotionally disturbed, she happened to do anything that broke the law. She replied, "I started a riot and slugged a counselor." This was at a previous school. I said, "Well, now I understand why you are here." I then shifted my emphasis and asked her with point-blank seriousness, "Are you going to do that at Ventura?" Probably my direct, honest question reached her because she immediately answered, "No, I don't think so, I like it here."

I asked her if she would like to come into my group therapy. She had already been selected for individual therapy by one of our psychologists because, on the basis of her previous record, she was potentially as difficult a girl as had ever been sent to us. Because of her bad record I decided she was worth a joint effort and also placed her in group therapy. Although the psychologist left Ventura after several months, he exerted a strong positive influence on her which helped greatly. Compared to Sharon, Linda's course at the school was uneventful. She left in December 1962 after a stay of about six months. Before she left I asked her to write a summary of her experiences in institutions and with psychiatric treatment. The following was written in December 1962 shortly before she left.

During the past three years I have been under a variety of psychotherapists and in this time I have experienced a number of different attitudes toward myself and towards those who surround me. My first psychiatrist was a rather large shoulder-to-cry-on type and I learned after a while that if there was something I wanted that my parents would normally have denied to me, then I could use her as an intercedent and it was almost sure that this request would be granted. She convinced me that I was emotionally disturbed and, therefore, was not to be held responsible for my actions. After I had been in the Juvenile Hall for the first time, I began to receive the therapy of an institutional nature and in this way I tended to get my way when I felt it was a subject that was worth getting "upset" over. Since it was on my record that I was an emotionally disturbed child, there were various exceptions made for me on this premise. I was not to be upset as I became violent and even masochistic at times. This eliminated the possibilities of the confinement unit; I would have been left alone there and would have been required to think and this was supposed to be bad for me. It was at this point in my life that I learned the advantages of being emotionally disturbed and I played them to the fullest advantage. I was upset a lot and managed to time these little episodes to get in or out of most of the difficulties that were encountered.

I then entered a school full of girls like myself who had been either in minor or major difficulties. They ranged from assault and prostitution cases to run-away and sex delinquency. But we were all upset quite often and found this to be a clear reason for anything we did. After all we were the emotionally disturbed and high strung delinquents and this made any and all we did excusable. We had both private and group therapy. These were sessions in which each girl relived all the frustrations and disturbances. We were allowed the excessive use of profanity, even when directed towards members of the staff. We were not required to give any of the respect their positions demanded. It was through these various therapy sessions that the girls managed to manipulate the staff into their way of thinking and would mold the rules to comply with what they wanted.

Shortly before my release from that institution I struck a staff member and instigated a riot which got me sent to California Youth Authority and found that these people had an extremely different attitude toward the girls. So you were emotionally disturbed, so big deal! There wasn't anything that anyone but you could do about it so why worry. I was there under the therapy of Dr. Glasser and Mr. Toobert. I found that Dr. Glasser was less interested in what you had done in your past than he was in your immediate and far future. He was a very personable man and he gave you the feeling that he was interested in you, but not what you had done, and never implied that there was any reason to ask why as there was no fact necessary but that you did it and that was the reason for your present incarceration. However, there was not any excuse for what you had done and you were to hold no one else responsible for your actions. This is good for it makes you accept the responsibility rather than give the fault to everyone who helped compose your environment. Now I am leaving Ventura Y. A. in a matter of days. I have learned that I cannot alter the past but can control my future and the responsibility lies solely with me as to my future.

Those who wonder what happens to girls after they leave the school will find the following letters very instructive.

January 16, 1963

Dear Dr. Glasser,

Hi! What's happening? Everything is fine here. I am in the process of having my tattoos out (my wrist, my hands, my right ankle, and my left calf are gone). The rest are steadily coming out. Pretty soon I'll look normal again! I am back in school again, Junior year. I still find myself thinking wrongly about the girls but hope I can change. I got a letter from Ted. I was engaged when I got busted and he says he still loves me and wants to marry me despite everything, but I am not ready to marry yet, so I won't. My brother and I are getting along groovey. He made a pass at me and I set him straight, quite even-temperedly, and he seemed to understand quite well. So now we act like most brothers and sisters. I don't lose my temper much any more and I've become drastically quiet. Good huh? Well, I've taken enough of your valuable time. Write if you have the time.

Always,
Linda

February 5, 1963

Dear Dr. Glasser,

Well, things are okay now. They did get a little hectic there for a while. One of the girls that I was involved with at the Hall called me and I melted. She left her home and decided that she wanted to come over here to see me, so I got a little scared and called my parole officer and told her what was happening. I then called her mother and told her that her daughter was here in Covina and that I would give her the necessary money to get home on and put her on the bus to Los Angeles, which I did. I then found out that she had forged a check in her mother's name for ten dollars and that her mother was going to try and catch it before it hit the bank. She did and was able to make it good, but somehow the authorities found out about it, and she is evidently busted again for forgery. She is then also most likely to show up at the fine institution that you so nobly serve.

If she does, Dr. Glasser, try to help her because she really needs the help. She is a very mixed up little girl and I guess she feels terribly insecure in her own right. I know that you can't work very many miracles like you performed with me but you can sure give it an honest, all-American try and help a girl that could eventually amount to something. That's that! I told my parole officer that I wrote to you and that you wrote me back and gave her the letter to read. She definitely approves and thinks it would be good if I could visit you at the school. She would even like to go if she can find the time. She is pretty swingin' in her own little way but isn't permissive.

She gave her sanction for Alice and me to see each other at any time and to go places together. I have been to her home three times and have talked to her innumerable times on the telephone. I am going to try the straight life for a while. I am not placing any guarantees but will try like hell. There is this boy I used to go with who is presently in Vacaville for possession of narcotics, but I know he won't drag me down and maybe I can raise him up to some extent.

I am beginning to think like one of those social workers but I can't help the fact. I have faced a certain amount of prejudice due to my former place of residence, like losing a job on this account. I have also learned to accept those things which I can not change. This is a most valuable lesson to me. Agreed? I miss the school to a certain extent but am really trying to make a go of this life on the streets. I am trying to take it as easy as possible, to be the person I wanted to be when I left the school. I will be too, so there. Let Jean [our department secretary] read this too if she is interested in it and, of course, dictate the answer to her. She is groovey too. I still refuse to accept her age and her grown children. I refuse, so put that into your pipe and puff a while. Well I should get to bed sometime within the next hour, so I will close for now with the best wishes for you and the group of seven girls that you found to replace me. I don't know if I like the idea of your letting someone else take my place in your therapeutic heart.

As always,
Linda

March 12, 1963

Dear Dr. Glasser,

Well, in three more days I will have been gone from your fine institution for three months. Be proud because you are one of the more instrumental people in this. I think that I can stay out this time and am now trying to keep busy to stop from being bored. That isn't too difficult as my mother's condition is such that any work is bad for her, thus leaving all the housework to me, but I'm glad.

I think in one of my past letters I did explain to you that there was a boy in Vacaville that I used to go with. This stud wrote me while I was in Norwalk and I didn't receive the letter until I was paroled from V. T. and then I got my parole officer's permission to correspond. He was paroled the 15th of January, and with permission from both of our parole officers we are able to see one another. I feel a lot more for him than I thought myself capable of for a stud, not love but it might be someday. He knows about me and my escapades and he understands, or at least claims to. I still harbor strong feelings for S. and D., but I think these will die as soon as their closeness in memory wears off.

Besides after considerable thought on the matter I don't think that a woman could make me happy for the rest of my life as I am too fond of children. I think that I will eventually marry some stud, be it this one or someone else. Aren't you proud of your forecasting, and the first "I told you so" I detect is going to aggravate me muchly. From the nitty gritty out here I understand that Tina is on her way up there. Please try to help her, Dr. Glasser. She needs help as she is confused and needs to be made to realize a lot of things and to stop harping on things that are past and unalterable. I guess that the time is ever present in her mind that her parents both contend that the other hates her, but constant harping on it isn't going to do anyone any good, most of all her. I think that she likes being in trouble because in her mind it makes her something big. I went through this too so I can understand this feeling. Please try to help her, for if anyone can it is you. See the faith I have in you. Well there isn't much else to say so I will close for now. God bless you and keep you safe, sound and healthy.

As always,
Linda

The following is a letter from Alice who was mentioned in the letter of February 5, 1963.

March 25, 1963

Dear Dr. Glasser,

I saw Linda today. She's changed even more so. Lacking her monopoly on mass-hysteria she's quieter, her hands have visibly ceased shaking, she is no longer obsessed with her various neuroses, and the tedious exhortations concerning her emotional disturbances have been replaced by a new kind of sensitivity. This sensitivity most amazes me because a year ago, before you, she was really the most self-centered, depressed, hostile and thoroughly miserable person I'd ever encountered. Furthermore her exceptionally high intelligence prompted a pure intellectualization of any and all situations she was confronted with, leaving her emotionally sterile—except for hate and fear of herself and the threat of an omnipotent society.

Of course I'm not suggesting that I was emotionally at peace but I liked my neurosis much better. Besides, I could see and cope with hers where mine appeared distant. The world is very big and suddenly she's not squashed in a corner fighting like a rat. She's really out there and the air is clean, the sun shines all day long, and cops and robbers is a game only children play. She smiles now often and the need to control, to play aggressor, to hold the deck isn't as compelling as it was. She can almost be a passive receptor in human relationships. Goodness, I should be a psychoanalyst! But though I've corrected many of my own private scenes and have obtained a great degree of happiness, I don't by any means consider myself knowing enough to be of much more value than just her friend.

Respectfully,
Alice

P. S. Linda and I are coming up to the school Thursday of Easter week.

The following are further letters from Linda.

March 27, 1963

Dear Dr. Glasser,

Well what's happening with you these days and how are the people who are still there? I hope that you and Jean are doing fine and that things are thawing out for you in the wing of the building. Thank her for her note on the bottom of your letter. It is nice to know that there are people who don't have to be who are interested in you. Also, thank you for saying that you will help Tina. It means a great deal to me. She isn't meant for this life any more than I am. I really hope that you can help her as much as you helped me.

The 22nd of April I am going to have all the rest of the tattoos taken out by a plastic surgeon and he will do it all in one fell swoop; thirteen holes in my leg and that will be the end of them for good. I am very happy. I have learned that one must accept the various foibles of society and tattoos on a girl shakes them up to no end. I wonder why?

I saw Alice. I have permission to see her from our parole officer Sunday and she sends her best. She is going to get married some time next month. Can you imagine her married so soon? I don't know if she is too wise in her decision but I sure wish her all the best in the world. There really isn't much happening here. I go to school every day and spend most of the rest of my day in homework or at work. In fact homework is what I should be doing now so I will get to it.

As always,
Linda

P. S. I have stopped swearing almost entirely.

May 6, 1963

Dear Dr. Glasser,

Just these few lines your way to let you know that I'm thinking about you and hope you are fine. You will never guess what, I am now tattooless! I don't have any more left to show I had any. The other three would have been too dangerous to remove so they left them. I am scarred pretty well, but at least I don't have signs all over me, and I can go to a public beach without feeling self-conscious. I am too glad.

Well it has been almost five months since I left your institution for good. Aren't you proud of me? I am good, huh? Bet you never thought I would make it this long. I didn't at least. There were those who agreed with this point of view. Guess I fooled them. You should have seen *Ben Hunter*[2] the other night. They were

---

[2] Ben Hunter moderates a local television panel show which attempts to discuss controversial subjects.

discussing homosexuality. One of the men was an old lady from the word go. He lives in Hollywood and feels that our government should be paternal in that they should control the sexual lives of everyone. Not only the deviates but everyone. He feels that if everyone doesn't fit into his little mold they are wrong. The second member was the minority leader in the California State Legislature. Man that guy was something else. He thought that we all owe something to society and in turn society owes us the protection of stringent sex laws. They were incidentally speaking of consenting adults.

On the other side of the fence was a woman lawyer who was all for the rights of free men. She felt that the sex life of an individual was his own business and no one else's. The fourth and final member was a very practical and good-type psychiatrist who thought that the deviate should be given medical help rather than stronger laws. It was quite a spirited debate.

Man, I spoke too soon. You see there is this broad. I pray to God that it is only a temporary infatuation, because if it ain't then I have finally jumped the fence. She totally fascinates me, her mind, her personality, her body, just her. Wow! I am too torn up, but I am trying to stay away from her. She is 20, soon to be 21. She is too pretty and too sweet, altogether wonderful. Maybe it is just a throw back, huh? I sure hope so, because this juggling I must do is too much. I am sure that she won't get me into trouble. She has never been in trouble herself. I am lost! For the first time in my life things are getting the best of me. I feel that I must get out for the best of everyone but there is no place to go. I don't love her yet! But man, I sure could without too much difficulty. I don't want to be homosexual. Well that's about it. Be good.

As always,
Linda

May 23, 1963

Dear Dr. Glasser,

Hi, what's happening to you these days? I have enclosed a picture of me taken about a month ago. Note the hairy eyebrows and the all-mine hair on my head. Pretty good huh? I felt awfully funny about being minus eyebrows when the norm was to have them. I mean the looks you get when the pencil has run or is all gone. There you stand looking like the lord high executioner. Wow! Tell Mr. Weist [Chief Psychologist at Ventura] that I see Betty with permission from our parole officer and that she is doing very well. Her halo isn't shining too well yet, but she is on her way. She is very paranoid still and she has this terrible feeling that Mrs. B. is trying to get something on her, but I think she will make it pretty well if she can make the next month or so. Her address is . . . if he wishes to write to her.

Well I look quite delinquent now. I am in Levis with a can of beer and a cigarette, but don't let that fool you cuz 'taint so. I am a confirmed ex-delinquent and shall stay that way. Just think, I turned 15 in the Temple City Jail and 16 in the Old School and I will turn 17 right here. Oh joyous days. The 15th of June I will have made it for six months. The 21st I will be 17. Pretty good huh? Just think, me 17. I never thought I would make it freeside, but I did. I have a job and am getting along in school very well. I am good, well cool anyway! I have been loaded only twice and that was right after I got out! See, I told ya so. Well there isn't much happening here, so I will close for a while.

Always,
Linda

P. S. When do you run away with me to Mexico?

Recently, in June 1964, I received an invitation to Linda's high school graduation and following that a letter saying that she was to be discharged from parole, eighteen months after she left Ventura. For a girl of her age, eighteen months is the minimum time for discharge.

When I wrote Linda and asked her permission to include her letters in this book, I received the following note:

August 12, 1964

Dr. Glasser,

Of course you have my permission to use the piece I wrote for you before I left and any or all of the letters I have written to you as long as my name is not used.

Mrs. Linda Jones

P. S. Will write you a letter later as there is much to tell you. I am married now! Think on that for a while. I ain't queer in any manner anymore! I gave up girls totally.

Some people might argue that she is a little young for marriage, but I am satisfied that she is much more mature than her years and that this is an extremely satisfactory result of the California Youth Authority program at Ventura and on parole.

CONCLUSION

Not all the problems that confront us in our attempt to practice Reality Therapy at Ventura can be described here. Jeri, Maria, Terry, Liz, Sharon, and Linda are representative of the most difficult girls who come there. Few are as smart and intuitively responsive as Jeri, Liz, and Sharon, few as deprived as Maria, or as temperamental as Liz. For all-around delinquent behavior Linda would rank near the top of anyone's list, but in each case the principles of good treatment remain the same. Each case must be treated individually, and good judgment must be exercised in the application of the principles of Reality Therapy.

This chapter has presented the bare bones of a very intense human treatment which is difficult to apply consistently to all the people who resist. Patience, strength, and responsibility are needed. When we fail it is because we have not had enough of all three. With enough treatment, there are only a few girls who cannot be helped to help themselves, but the process requires great effort and much time.

If one is looking for easy answers to the problems of delinquency, I can offer no panacea; but if one is looking for an answer that will work, given enough time, energy, and concern, Reality Therapy can often do the job.

We believe that with training and experience we can become more efficient, but the job will never be easy, and there will always be failures. The failures, however, will be no mystery; we can always go back over the case and find the time that we did not maintain the involvement, did not control, did not insist upon responsibility and, therefore, *did not care.*

SOME PERTINENT RESEARCH ON THE
PSYCHIATRIC TREATMENT OF DELINQUENTS

In psychiatry, opinion concerning the effectiveness of various therapies is far more common than verification through a reasonably controlled research program. It is easy to state that Reality

Therapy is a better treatment than more traditional approaches, but it is much more difficult to demonstrate it.

As much as Dr. Harrington and I would like to verify our method by other means beyond comparison with seemingly similar situations, neither of us is in a position to set up a controlled research program. In appropriating money for psychiatric treatment in the California Youth Authority, however, the state legislature requested the Youth Authority Division of Research to assess whether or not the treatment of the most seriously disturbed wards by psychiatrists, psychologists, and social workers was effective.

In doing so the treatment program was assessed at two schools, one for younger boys of fourteen and fifteen, the other for older boys of seventeen and eighteen. The primary conclusion drawn from the study came as a great surprise to the research staff, and is quoted:

> If the treatment approaches at the two schools are indeed as described by staff, it is evident that we were not evaluating the Youth Authority Psychiatric Treatment Program at two institutions but rather two very different psychiatric treatment programs, one of which apparently helped to make wards less delinquent, and one of which may have promoted delinquent behavior.

This is indeed an interesting finding. Psychiatric treatment apparently is not a specific entity, but rather, at least in these schools, consists of two very different programs, both of which are called psychiatric treatment. Let us consider the main result of the study which led to the above conclusion, and then quote the researcher concerning the differences she found when the startling results caused her to examine the programs themselves. To quote again:

> By the criterion of violation of parole within 15 months, the effect of the younger boys' treatment program was significantly better than the effect of the older boys' treatment program. This was a result of appreciably *more parole violations* among the older boys' experimentals than controls.

That is, in each school a group needing treatment was selected. The group was then divided in half at random. One half, called *experimentals,* received psychiatric treatment. The other half, called *controls,* went through the program without treatment. In the case of the younger boys, treatment helped significantly; but in the case of the older boys, treatment did significant harm to their chances of success on parole.

Another finding of interest concerned the effect of treating boys of different maturity: "Low maturity boys at the older boys' school violated parole at an appreciably higher rate if they were in treatment than if they were not. High maturity boys did not show any difference." This means that those boys initially assessed as having low maturity (boys that we would call highly irresponsible) were harmed by the treatment, whereas the high maturity (less irresponsible) boys were not. The only conclusion one can draw is that the kind of treatment used did not affect the more responsible boys, but that it played havoc with those who ordinarily need treatment urgently, the least responsible boys.

The next question that may be asked is: Were the younger boys better risks, that is, were they considered to be more amenable to treatment and more mature for their age? To answer this question we quote again: "It was found that the younger boys had a disproportionately larger number of poor risks and smaller number of good risks than did the older boys. . . . On the basis of these data one would expect the younger boys' group to have a higher violation rate than the older boys."

Therefore, the difference in favor of the treatment results in the younger boys' school was not because they were better parole risks. In fact, it was just the opposite. Could it be that younger boys are generally easier to treat than older boys? Here again we quote the author: "We also know that one group was older, but offhand one would hypothesize that this was to the advantage of the older boys insofar as they might be expected to be better able to understand and to conceptualize their problems."

To summarize, after examining all of the known differences between the groups at each school, the author concludes: "In short, none of the known differences between the wards at the two schools would have led one to expect a differential effect of treatment in favor of the younger boys." The researcher then goes on to ask and to try to answer the critical question raised by this study in which one program helped the boys treated and the other did them significant harm. To quote:

Next we ask ourselves, were the psychiatric treatment programs themselves different at the two schools? During the experiment the Research Division was not aware of any factors operating at the two schools which might have prepared them for the finding that the younger boys' school program would be significantly better.

In looking for the difference, the researcher interviewed the staffs and found a major difference in philosophy:

At the younger boys' school several members of the treatment staff emphasized the ward's responsibility for his own behavior and minimized psychodynamics or psychosocial etiology of the ward's emotional disturbance or delinquent behavior. This approach may have been more acceptable to custody staff both because it was less esoteric and because its goal, *responsible behavior,* was similar to theirs.

In contrast:

The staff at the older boys' school feels that since the treatment goals and the techniques used for achieving these are of the more classical type, more time was needed than the usual stay permitted. Uncovering, interpreting, reflecting and working through both the positive and the negative transference require a great deal of time. Still more time would be needed before insight could be assimilated and translated into behavioral changes. It was felt that the necessarily premature termination of therapy might have left the patient more vulnerable than before.

From the last two quotations it is apparent that some staff members at the school that produced good results practiced an approach similar to the Reality Therapy we use at Ventura. At the other school, the traditional concepts of psychotherapy seemed to do more harm than good in the time allotted for treatment.

We take the most difficult girls into treatment and we would not be surprised if they did not measure up to the average success of our whole program. Rather than emphasize treated versus non-treated girls which at Ventura would be an artificial separation, it would be much more valid to measure our total program against a girls' school where traditional concepts prevail. The Youth Authority research staff is aware of our Reality Therapy program and agrees that such a comparison could be made.

4 | Hospital Treatment of Psychotic Patients

The application of Reality Therapy to the treatment of long-term hospitalized psychotic patients is examined in this chapter. The hospital is the Veterans Administration Neuropsychiatric Hospital in West Los Angeles, the building is 206, and the physician in charge is Dr. G. L. Harrington.

Building 206, composed of four wards totaling 210 patients, has been in existence for almost twenty years at the V.A. hospital. Until recently, when Dr. Harrington introduced the concepts of Reality Therapy, it housed the most chronic, stable, psychotic patients in the hospital. It had the traditional mental hospital approach in which the patients were accepted as mentally ill and were given good standard care. Any active treatment, however, was oriented toward helping them maintain themselves at as high a level as possible *within the hospital*. No dramatic change in their condition was expected and the average discharge rate was about two patients a year. The patients' problems were categorized into the standard, meaningless, hospital diagnoses: paranoid schizophrenia, catatonic schizophrenia, hebephrenic schizophrenia, and the old wastebasket diagnosis of chronic, undifferentiated schizophrenia. Labeled with these anti-therapeutic terms, the patients did about what was expected of them. They hallucinated a little, suffered from a few delusions, but mostly they sat around in the relatively plush V.A. mental hospital environment waiting out their lives. Most patients stayed in the ward indefinitely; fifteen years was the average length of stay in Building 206.

Here over 210 men lived separated from the world, both through their own choice, and by the traditional mental illness concepts which prevailed there and still prevail in most mental hospitals. Symbiosis had been established. The patients were no longer actively crazy, they needed little care, and the hospital accepted them as mentally ill people who had arrived at their permanent station in life. For all practical purposes, a contract had been signed that both sides were scrupulous in fulfilling.

It was this contract, the concurrence of the staff with the patients' agreement to stay peacefully psychotic, that Dr. Harrington broke when he took over the ward in 1962. Stepping down at his own request from an administrative position, he returned to his more congenial post of ward physician. Completely in charge of Building 206, he introduced a total Reality Therapy program into the lives of the staff and patients with the help of one social worker and one psychologist.

The impact of the new program quickly began to show on the ward. Increasing numbers of patients began to be discharged. A few at first, and then at a steadily ascending rate, the releases climbed from the average of two per year to twenty-five in 1962. In 1963, seventy-five patients were released with only three returning. Dr. Harrington now estimates that over the next few years this rate will climb to approximately two hundred a year, which means a complete turnover of the ward each year.

The spectacular increase in discharge rate has been accomplished with less psychiatric time devoted to the ward than before. Dr. Harrington, replacing a full-time psychiatrist, spends only twenty hours a week at the hospital; the rest of the staff has remained the same. The average patient has spent an increasing number of years in mental hospitals because the emptied beds are continually filled by the almost inexhaustible supply of veterans transferred from state hospitals. A veteran whose disability is not service-connected is eligible for V.A. care when there are no veterans with service-connected disabilities requesting admission. The average transferee has been a patient in a state hospital for over fifteen years. Men who have been hospitalized for twenty years are not uncommon as it is now twenty-four years since the draft began in 1940.

As it was in the Ventura School for Girls, the first and perhaps most important step in applying Reality Therapy in Building 206 was to convince each staff member that, because it is a total program he is just as important to the success of the program as is the ward psychiatrist. Dr. Harrington carefully taught and retaught each staff member to forget the concept of schizophrenia and mental illness, and to consider the patients as people who are behaving this way because that is the best they have been able to do up to now. He instructed them, however, not to respond to the abnormal behavior and thinking, but to treat each patient as if he is capable of not being crazy now; in this ward he does not have to be.

Every staff member is taught that, at one time in his life, each long-term patient had been unable to fulfill his needs and was, therefore, unable to function in a responsible manner. Because he could not fulfill his needs in the real world, sometimes suddenly but more often gradually, the patient began to deny the existence of the real world and live in a world of his own, trying thereby to fulfill his needs. Perhaps it was a completely crazy world full of hallucinations and delusions; perhaps it was just a numb denial of reality and a withdrawal into a world of nothingness, a vegetative existence in which the patient goes through only the bare motions of life. No matter what his behavior, it was his way of trying to fulfill his needs or denying that he had needs to fulfill. Sooner or later someone began to notice that he was acting peculiarly. If he was grossly disturbed he was immediately hospitalized, but often he gradually drifted into a world of his own and on into the hospital.

Once hospitalized, however, no matter how the patient behaved he was accepted as mentally ill, according to the usual teachings of modern psychiatry. He was considered to be suffering from a psychotic reaction for which he needed help. In many fortunate cases the psychosis was self-limited. In the easy, accepting atmosphere of a good hospital the patient became more comfortable, his symptoms lessened, and he returned to our world—to reality—and was discharged. His psychosis was no longer present because he could again fulfill his needs. This sequence is common for about half of those who leave reality, and their treatment is comparatively easy. Removed from the stressful conditions of the outside world, these patients quickly gain strength and reconstitute themselves. They may relapse again; but if their world is a little less stressful, as it may be because less is now expected of them, and with the strength gained in the hospital, they often have no further psychotic episodes.

The major difficulty occurs with the half who do not respond to traditional hospital treatment. They do not quickly return to reality in the protected environment of the hospital. Rather, they adjust; that is, they decide that it is safer or easier to fulfill their needs in the hospital than it was wherever they came from or than it will be wherever they may possibly go, so they continue to be psychotic, to deny the world. Although they may give up all or some of their crazy symptoms in the hospital, any effort to move them out of the hospital causes the symptoms to return, so they stay, becoming citizens of the world of the mental hospital. Varying in behavior from almost complete contact with reality to extreme disorganization, they remain about the same for years. No one then really thinks they will improve as the first group did, which usually takes about six months. After about three years they are shifted to a holding building, as 206 used to be, and given little hope. Unless something dramatic or unusual happens, they will die unchanged.

The above description well fitted Building 206 before Reality Therapy was introduced. Now, however, the staff has been trained to understand that there is a better world for the patients than the world of the mental hospital. They have been thoroughly instructed that they must never accept the situation as hopeless, that each patient can be taught better ways to act, and that there is some place for him in the world. The staff of Building 206 no longer believe that mental illness exists; the patients can, therefore, do better if they can be helped to help themselves *slowly but surely act more responsibly.* Toward this end, Dr. Harrington has set up a specific program, one that is remarkably similar in principle to the program at Ventura School.

THE PROGRAM OF BUILDING 206

Prior to 1962, Building 206 was known as the chronic or "crock" ward. All patients had received therapy of various kinds without success and had been sent to Building 206 for custodial care. The building was an open ward with off-building privileges but few off-building responsibilities. Because it was so easy to live in the hospital, there was little incentive to change. Tender, loving care was the order of the day. Off-building privileges, passes into town, passes home for weekends, Thanksgiving, Christmas, and the Fourth of July were considered to be every patient's dream. All patients' requests and demands were fulfilled whenever possible, a marked difference from any world they would have to live in if they left.

Group therapies were organized around the principle of making conscious the unconscious in the traditional sense. The great insight into their "illness" that many patients obtained did not increase their responsibility. When they understood why they were mentally ill, it made even more sense to them to stay as they were.

Dr. Harrington instituted the Reality Therapy program when he took over Building 206. Rather than concentrating on making the patient happy, the program stressed carefully graded increments of responsibility so that the patient could slowly work his way back to reality. The building was divided into a fifty-man closed ward, a fifty-man semi-open ward, and a one hundred-man open ward. All personnel, including clerk-typist, clothing-room clerk, aides, nurses, social worker, and psychologist, were given responsibilities of reporting behavior concerning the patients' readiness for movement either in the direction of greater or lesser responsibility. During a regular building meeting attended by both staff and patients, patient problems were discussed, ward assignments were made (usually along the progression from closed to semi-open to open ward status), and individual patient programs were established. The results of all meetings were typed and placed on the patients' bulletin boards.

On the day the program was put into force, Dr. Harrington had a forty-five-second meeting with the least responsible and most crazy patients, who had been selected for the closed ward. The patients were told simply that in the doctor's judgment they needed a rest on the closed ward as they were not yet ready for the open ward. At the conclusion of the meeting, one patient raised his hand and asked the doctor if he could have a pass into town. When the request was denied, he said, "Thank you, Doctor."

As Dr. Harrington left the ward, a patient who was evidently disturbed because he was left in open status approached him, asking if he could be transferred to Building 205, the maximum security ward. Dr. Harrington asked him if he had not been selected to be placed on the closed ward. The patient said no, as far as he knew he was still an open status, to which Dr. Harrington responded, "You're on closed status now." The patient shook hands and said, "Thank you," and the program was under way. It is Dr. Harrington's contention that patients recognize their need for closed status even more acutely than does the staff, as was demonstrated by his exchange with the last patient.

Critics have argued that the procedures of Reality Therapy would make no sense to the patients after all their years of hospital life. In practice such criticism proved to be invalid, further bolstering our conviction that mental illness does not exist. The patients sensed from the total ward attitude that something new was happening, that someone really cared, and that they were involved in a very different hospital experience than any they had had before. In the locked ward, patients who were violent or destructive were put in a belt and cuffs because crazy behavior is not tolerated. Hyperactive patients were given sedation. The aides and nurses worked toward becoming involved with the patients and then asked them to give up their crazy symptoms.

The involvement now becomes critical. The men selected for the closed ward were those least involved with others and most isolated from reality. Here the aides and nurses engage in a continual therapeutic effort to involve the patient first with them and then with the minimum closed ward program. In a totally accepting, protected atmosphere, the ward staff use patience, humor, and persistence to force themselves into the patient's life. Attaining the initial involvement takes anywhere from a few weeks to as long as six months, but sooner or later the effort by the ward staff begins to show. The patient responds either by increasing his symptoms or by decreasing them and thus changing to more reasonable behavior. In either case his response shows that the first part of therapy, the initial involvement, has been accomplished.

Now the attitude can be changed toward continued acceptance of the patient but rejection of the symptoms. For the first time in years the patients genuinely respond to human efforts. Those who show an increase in symptoms are trying to avoid involvement, but this behavior indicates that they are already beginning to be involved. In addition they may be testing the intent and persistence of the ward staff, for many therapists had tried in the past to get them involved, but they had not devoted enough time or effort, nor had they worked in the proper closed ward atmosphere. Little attention is paid to an increase in symptoms or to withdrawal, and these patients soon change their response and begin to give up their symptoms.

The final step on the closed ward is to help the patients begin to function; that is to eat, bathe, shave, brush their teeth, change clothes, and take needed medicine. Even in cuffs they are expected to take some responsibility for their personal care, awkward as it might be. Available but not required of patients are television, ward games, and a weekly trip to the canteen accompanied by an aide. When they can perform the minimum functions, the patients no longer need cuffs and sedation. When they are able to act sensibly most of the time they are ready for step two.

Recommendations for a patient to move to the semi-open ward are made by the staff at the building meeting, although Dr. Harrington makes all the decisions and the patients know this. He becomes a vital part of their world, and it is his training and judgment that the patients, as well as the staff, learn to depend on. They trust him not to move them until they are ready, yet they strive for progress because they can and do understand that the Reality Therapy program is the start of a new life for them. *It is the whole ward attitude, where everyone is involved, but where mental illness is not accepted, that brings the understanding home to them.*

Between two and six months are usually needed to prepare

patients for the semi-open ward where they are told that they must stay in the ward although it is not locked. Here they are expected to attend a group meeting run by aides in which their responsibility within the ward program is discussed. Adding at least an hour of ward detail to their closed ward duties, they are slowly but surely given increased responsibility and told that they now have an opportunity to make progress.

By taking steadily increasing responsibility, they begin to gain self-respect and self-worth. Now they are easier for the staff to like and thus they are more likely to fulfill their need for love. They start to feel better and to look and act like men, not like permanent mental hospital residents. Next they get a ground privilege card which entitles them to go outside but which carries with it the obligation to do an outside work detail. Emphasis continues on constructive, realistic work activity. Patients do not wander the grounds as docile inmates, nor do they engage in play or "therapeutic" make work aimed at making them happy. The goal is to return them to reality, not to make them well adjusted to hospital life. Soon they are ready to go off grounds with the family, if it is judged to be beneficial. Later in the semi-open ward program, patients may go to off-building activities and have off-ground passes, both accompanied and unaccompanied.

In contrast to therapy on the closed ward, which is essentially continuous, therapy now becomes more structured. An important part of the new program is a daily meeting of a therapy group led by an aide trained in Reality Therapy in which the patients discuss their progress in detail. Here they experience the good feeling that results from expressing themselves in a group. All the problems of taking responsibility are patiently and repeatedly gone over as the initial involvement gained in the closed ward is expanded. Relearning how to live in the world beyond the ward for short periods, the patient is carefully prepared for the measured increase in responsibility of each step. The doctor uses his judgment to regulate the speed of the process.

Because it has been discovered that the patient is usually ready to move downstairs to a completely open ward in about ninety days, this time limit is made a condition of the group on the semi-open ward. Downstairs the patient enters another time-limited group led by either a social worker or a psychologist specially trained in Reality Therapy, who actively prepares groups of patients for the next step, the move out of the hospital. Setting time limits of ninety days motivates the patients to work harder toward the goal of leaving. If they do not succeed in ninety days, they are moved back; but well over 90 per cent do succeed. Dr. Harrington believes that those who succeed should increase to almost 100 per cent as everyone learns more about applying the principles of Reality Therapy.

Patients who cannot manage the rapid movement are moved backwards, even to the locked ward. Such regression is neither failure nor admission that the craziness was too well established, but rather a sign that the ward doctor had erred in his judgment. The patient in his characteristic way communicates his feelings by acting crazy or irresponsible. But whether or not regression occurs, movement generally continues forward.

Now downstairs in the open ward, with many privileges earned by taking responsibility, the patient is deeply involved with the program because he knows that in three months he must leave the hospital. The social worker or psychologist leads the group in learning how to live without the protection of the hospital. Entering a carefully planned outside situation, the patient in many cases returns during the day to work and to receive the support of the hospital program; however, he is primarily dependent upon himself.

When a patient is finally moved out to his family, a foster home, an apartment (or, if he is old and feeble, to the old soldiers' home), he is instructed not to look for work. In the beginning, after ten or twenty years in the hospital, it is enough just to leave. Work comes later. To expect too much too soon from men who have been separated so long from the real world will produce a return of irresponsible behavior. Timing and judgment are critical; but if the patient is not yet ready, he can retrace as many steps as necessary—just as a girl who can't succeed on parole returns to the school as a part of a continuing program which in the end will produce permanently increased responsibility.

Building 206 sets a standard for proper treatment of chronic mental patients. Its program takes less money and less time than do traditional methods, but it does demand a high degree of skill and training for the staff. Vital to the program on Building 206 but difficult to describe are the detailed plans and the intricate personal relationships which help each man to move over critical hurdles. The ability of the doctor to make the correct decisions, to time each move properly, is part of the skill of psychiatry learned only through experience.

A strikingly similar program, described at the end of this chapter, works well for newly admitted hospital patients to prevent them from arriving at the chronic "adjusted" stage that the veterans arriving in Building 206 have unfortunately attained. By preventing long separations from the real world, the road back can be shorter and easier to travel; but as long as the traditional mental illlness concepts prevail, Building 206 will be the exception. Time devoted to programs other than sensitively retraining patients to be responsible will neither prevent half of all admissions from becoming chronic patients nor bring back to reality those who do become chronic. Millions of dollars will continue to be spent to investigate the causes of a nonexistent disease, mental illness, to find answers already graphically demonstrated in Building 206. The same money spent in other hospitals to set up similar programs would return a much greater dividend. But the mental illness concept is deeply entrenched in mental hospitals, and it will take public pressure to change it. Psychiatry is seemingly too close to the problem to take action itself.

ROY

Roy is an example of a patient who has been in both the old and new programs in Building 206.[1]

By midsummer of 1944, Roy was finished with the war in Europe. He was twenty-four years old, with a left leg three-quarters as good as new. He had come through a particular man-made kind of hell with flying colors. The not remarkably proud possessor of the Purple Heart and a personal citation for heroism, he felt that he had done only what the circumstances called for. Whatever was heroic about it had to do with the time, the place, and the minds of

[1] The description of Roy and a critical appraisal in Chapter 6 was contributed by Dr. G. L. Harrington.

other people. His widowed mother was not surprised at his hero-ism because, as she put it, "He'd been the man of the house since he was eight years old, when his father died."

He had never been a problem as a child, helping to care for the three younger children. At ten (two years younger than any other paper-carrier in the home town) he had acquired a paper route, and for the next seven years he never failed to get up at 4 A.M., winter or summer, to carry his papers. He turned his weekly $5 paycheck over to his mother for the family fund. He made good grades in school. No, his mother was not surprised at his heroism for she knew that he would always conduct himself properly and do right, no matter what the situation was.

Just two days before Roy was to board a ship to return to the States, it happened without warning. He ran amuck. He was cap-tured by guards as he ran through the hospital compound, scream-ing that the Nazis were pouring in the south gate and crying out orders for hand grenades and bayonets. Some of his bunk mates remembered that he had been pacing around the ward more than usual and that he probably hadn't slept too well for a few nights, but no one could believe what was happening to this mild-man-nered, quiet, considerate member of their group.

In the psychiatric unit Roy was grossly disturbed, requiring heavy sedation. Obviously hallucinating, he heard voices accusing him of being a homesexual; he lashed out at the voices continu-ously, smashing his head and his hands through walls, doors, and windows. After several days' observation it was concluded that the patient was suffering from dementia praecox (paranoid type) acute, manifested by ideas of reference, delusions of persecution, and hallucinations. Shortly thereafter he was started on a course of electric shock treatment. After fifteen treatments he had improved enough to allow the therapy to be stopped. At the end of one month the patient appeared to be in a state of good remission. Unable to remember exactly what had happened, he spoke of it all as a bad dream.

Six weeks after the onset of his acute illness the patient was discharged from the service, going to his mother's home in the Midwest. When he arrived home he had changed. According to his mother, he wasn't the boy she had known. He had no interest in the house or his younger brother and two sisters. He paced the floor, did not sleep for three nights, and on the fourth day had to be corraled by the local police for smashing furniture and windows. Hospitalized on an acute, intensive treatment service in a local V.A. hospital for the next three months, he received forty electric shock treatments with what were considered to be excellent results. The patient was anxious to leave the hospital to go home to pick up where he had left off before the war. His mother, realizing something was still wrong, nevertheless insisted on taking him home and doing everything she could to help him back to health. He was at home ten days before another psychotic episode occurred. This time taken to another V.A. hospital in the area, his treatment again began on the acute, intensive treatment service. The patient, very disturbed, was kept in seclusion. Before preparations for him to receive insulin coma treatment were finished, his acute episode subsided, and the staff decided to withhold this form of therapy.

Within six weeks Roy appeared to be in a state of fair remission. He was transferred from the acute service to an open convalescent service where he could receive psychotherapy. Two hours after his arrival on the open service he became acutely psychotic, with hallucinations and his old destructive behavior. Returned first to the acute, intensive treatment service, where his symptoms subsided within a week, he was transferred to a closed, chronic service for custodial care.

During the next four years Roy made only a marginal adjustment to the ward routine. Spending most of his time sitting, looking off into space, he did not communicate or otherwise socialize with other patients. On direct questioning by his ward doctor, he just answered the questions, offering nothing to the conversation. When asked whether he heard voices, he replied that he did; when asked what they told him, he said they called him a queer; when asked where the voices came from, he said he wasn't sure but he thought it was some Nazi organization.

In 1950 the patient escaped from the hospital. For the next four years nothing was known of his whereabouts, although later his mother reported that he had visited home briefly in 1952, but again disappeared. Recently, he revealed that he had spent these four years wandering around the country.

In 1954 he was picked up by the Los Angeles police, disheveled, confused, and totally disoriented. When it was discovered that he was a veteran, he was transferred from Los Angeles County Hospital to the local V.A. hospital, where he was placed on the acute, intensive treatment service. His new doctor, a first-year resident, was a warm, kindly, born-to-be-a-doctor young man who read the glassy, distant stare in Roy's eyes as fear. Roy must have sensed his doctor's warmth and interest, for almost immediately he began to follow the doctor's instructions by eating better, keeping cleaner, and improving his appearance. Completely oriented within a month, he had gained ten pounds and was busy making ash trays for the ward in the occupational therapy shop.

Shortly thereafter, his doctor decided to see Roy in individual psychotherapy. The conduct of the therapy was supervised by an experienced psychoanalyst who was a consultant to the residence training program. The sessions between the resident and his supervisor dealt with helping the young psychiatrist gain a deeper understanding of the structures of the mind (the super-ego, the ego, and the id), the principles of psychosexual development, the relationship between latent homosexuality and paranoid schizophrenia, and techniques for helping patients solve intrapsychic conflicts by means of insight into unconscious impluses. Roy's therapy progressed rapidly and satisfactorily. Deeply interested in what his doctor had to say, he offered much to the therapy in terms of feelings, thoughts, and memories from his past life. He spent much time when not in therapy thinking about his new-found knowledge of the mind, and once offered a possible fifth proposition to Freud's original four propositions concerning the mechanism for the development of paranoia to ward off homosexuality.

Roy's progress in understanding was equally impressive to himself, to his doctor, and to his doctor's supervisor. Finally, after eight months of intensive work, the doctors agreed that he was no longer schizophrenic, that he was a sensitive, stable human being ready to take his place in the world. At his supervisor's suggestion, the resident doctor told the patient of the conclusions and wrote an order transferring him to an open ward from which he would soon be discharged. Thirty minutes after he arrived on the open ward he was screaming out loudly against the voices and had to be restrained; he was placed in seclusion on the closed unit. The resident, a most distraught young man, declared that everything had gone along perfectly until the damn voices came back and spoiled everything, as if the voices were in truth a visitation from outer space.

Roy's destructive, disturbed behavior could not be controlled on the acute, intensive treatment service and he was, therefore, transferred to a maximum security ward. Although his acute episode subsided the day after his arrival on the maximum security ward, he communicated with no one and did no more than meet the basic demands of the ward. His former resident doctor visited him once before moving to another service, but Roy did not recognize him.

By 1957, two years later, Roy was adjusting well to the ward routine, including participating in the occupational therapy program. His mother, who had now raised the other children and moved to California to be near her son, visited regularly on visiting days. There was little conversation between them, but the meetings appeared to be quietly pleasant. On occasions she would bring a picnic lunch and they would eat together on the grounds.

During 1958 it was concluded that the patient's psychosis had stabilized at as high a level as he could attain, and that he might be able to live in a family care home if it were a well-organized, protective environment. His mother was not happy to have him go to someone else's home, but agreed to it hoping it would help her son. Roy stayed in the home three days, became tense, and complained that the voices were returning. Although he did not become destructive, he insisted that he had to return to the hospital. Back at the V.A. hospital he remained in the maximum security building until the fall of 1960, when he was transferred to Building 206 for custodial care.

During the first three months in Building 206, the patient made a satisfactory adjustment to the closed ward. He spoke only when spoken to and did not socialize with other patients, yet seemed rather complacent and satisfied with his condition. Later, placed on an open ward and given certain hospital privileges, he was assigned to corrective therapy, a program aimed at sponsoring interplay between patients in team sports such as volleyball and basketball. After about a year in the program the patient had changed little in his ability to mix with people. He did what he was told and no more.

At this time Dr. Harrington took over Building 206 and started Reality Therapy. Roy was presented to the weekly building staff meeting on the insistence of the corrective therapy worker, who complained that he was unable to get anywhere with him. He behaved as if he were vegetating, and the corrective therapy worker wanted a re-evaluation of the patient's status and program. The building psychiatrist was taken aback when Roy walked into the room, well-groomed, composed, dignified, an early middle-aged man. The greeting was cordial, the handshake firm, and the silence that followed was forever until the doctor asked the patient how long he had been on corrective therapy. The response was a quick "Twelve months." Another pause, and the doctor asked how long he had been bored with corrective therapy. With the impassive face of a straight man, the patient responded "Eleven months." The room broke up in laughter matched in warmth only by Roy's restrained smile. He was then told that his activity was going to be changed from corrective therapy to the sidewalk detail, which consisted of digging, placing forms, mixing concrete, and pouring concrete for new sidewalks about the hospital grounds. Believing that he was not responsible enough for open status even though he was now tolerating it, Dr. Harrington moved Roy back to semi-open status on the second floor. Asked for his opinion of the changes, Roy said that he thought it was a good idea.

This three-minute interview signaled the breakthrough, small as it was, which started Roy in Reality Therapy. Until then he had been a patient in a hospital which was trying very hard to do something for him. In the past, when Roy seemed better it had meant only that he had accepted what the hospital was doing for him, whether it was shock treatment or psychoanalysis. He was mentally ill and he was being treated. When he became quiet and apparently rational his acceptance of the status quo was interpreted wrongly to mean that he was ready to leave the hospital. Each time, however, he was no more ready to fulfill his needs than before, so he behaved irrationally to emphasize how unready he was.

After years of the same reaction to the same program in various guises, he reached the point where he was vegetating in corrective therapy. Still unable to fulfill his needs in corrective therapy, he had now even given up trying to accept what was being done for him. To say that Roy was bored was a masterpiece of understatement, but in doing so Dr. Harrington showed recognition of his predicament and started their involvement. Roy sensed that here was a doctor who knew that there must be a better life for him than the one he was living, and he certainly knew that he had been at a dead end.

The initial involvement would have gone for naught had not Dr. Harrington given him less responsibility by moving him from the open to the semi-open ward. In the past when contact was made, Roy had been pushed ahead; now the opposite occurred. Roy could only interpret this change as understanding, caring, and acceptance. Instead of reacting with irrational fear, he was able to get into the new program of Building 206 as an active participant. Recreation was finally over; he accepted the assignment of working as a part of a crew building a concrete sidewalk, and he remained in the ward when he was not working. Except for the work, little was expected of him unless he himself asked for more responsibility. In group therapy led by a 206 aide he was given a chance to talk of what he was doing now, but he was not pushed to do more. If anything he was restrained; any push would have to come from him.

This treatment was new to Roy. When, as soon occurred, he sought out the doctor and asked for more freedom, he was told to wait. "You are not ready," was Dr. Harrington's refrain over and over again for the next two months. Although Roy asked for more freedom, he was really testing whether his new doctor would fail by granting him freedom before he was ready to fulfill his needs, as had happened so many times in the past. On the ward and at work his aides and nurses were friendly and interested in what he was now doing. They gave him praise but they did not push. On the job, however, he demonstrated his capability and was promoted to foreman of the sidewalk crew. Especially helpful in starting new men on the job, he showed real skill in taking this additional responsibility.

After about three months on the semi-open ward, Roy was very changed. Now it was not only Roy who was pushing Dr. Harrington; he was joined in his efforts by the aides and nurses. Increasingly involved with Roy and impressed by his progress, they began to badger Dr. Harrington to move him to the open ward and into a discharge group. This occurrence, when both staff and patients join together to press for more responsibility, is a critical point on the semi-open ward. When this joint push occurs it is the time to move the patient. If only the patient or only the staff urge a change, it is too early. Dr. Harrington resisted until the pressure grew intense, and then he told Roy that he was ready to take a Sunday pass to Santa Monica and report the following day to talk over how it went.

On Monday, Roy reported that he had done some window shopping in town. He was amazed at prices. He had eaten lunch on the pier, watched others fish, and had taken a sightseeing ride along the beach in a little bus. He enjoyed the outing and would like to repeat it regularly. The following week he was transferred from the second floor to the open ward on the first floor. Anticipating the outbursts he had had previously when he was put on open status, Dr. Harrington told him that it might be frightening, but that he thought he could make it. His program outside the building would remain the same and the personnel on the first floor knew him well. If the change proved to be too much for him, he would simply return to the second floor. During his first three days on the first floor, Roy seemed a bit preoccupied and a little distant, and he requested to see the doctor about some vague difficulties in swallowing. Without showing apprehension, Dr. Harrington treated him routinely. He was given some aspirin for his throat and reassured that he could make it on the open ward.

During the next two months the patient's work record on the sidewalk detail continued to improve. He was actively involved in the open ward therapy group which was directed toward planning to leave the hospital. Encouraged by everyone, he continued to take day passes to Santa Monica each week, accompanying other, more fearful patients on their first outing. Finally, it was decided that Roy should be seen in the staff meeting as a possible candidate for the day hospital program. His mother had been impressed by his progress; nevertheless, she feared the future and worried about his leaving the hospital on unaccompanied day passes. She sought out the building social worker and doctor many times, both of whom attempted to clarify for her the program in Building 206. She did not interfere in his day passes and she continued visiting, but now only one day a week, during visiting hours.

At the interview that decided whether or not Roy would go into the day hospital program, he was first asked what he saw for himself in the future. He declared that when we felt he was ready to leave the hospital he would go and live with his mother. He was told that because of his history and his own experience the staff had a different plan in mind. The day hospital program, in which a patient is placed on trial separation from the hospital, was explained. Finding himself a place to live near the hospital, he would return by day to continue his same hospital program. Again the responsibility was slowly and carefully extended.

Following this explanation, Roy paused and then admitted that he had escaped previously from a hospital and tried to make it on his own, but he had been unable to do so. The difference between that experience and his present program was discussed. In addition he was told that if he were selected for the day hospital program, he would be placed in a discharge group with the building social worker. Meeting twice a week for three months, the group would discuss the problems of living outside of the hospital.[2] The interview was concluded by Dr. Harrington telling the patient to think about the new program for another week and then to come to the staff meeting for a final decision on whether or not he would enter the program.

During the week the patient explained the whole program to his mother. After discussing it at length with the social worker, she gave her approval. At the staff meeting the following week, Roy said that he would like to try the program, and he was assigned to it.

[2] This was before the present modification of the program where as soon as the patient is moved to open status he goes into a ninety-day discharge group.

A total of twenty-three patients from Building 206 have been placed in the three-month treatment program for living outside the hospital and working in. The building psychologist has one therapy group and the social worker has two. Both leaders report that they are having a hilarious time. Some patients moan that it can't be done; others use the newspaper to quote prices on penthouses in Beverly Hills as evidence that a man with a pension can't afford to live outside the hospital. All are going on passes to look for places to live. Some want to move now and not wait three months. Roy has surveyed the local area with a fine-tooth comb, and has a file on rentals that would be the envy of any local rental office. They have discussed and checked the price of food and compared cooking in with eating out. Roy's group has enrolled en masse in a cooking school program offered by the hospital dietetics department. One group member excused the building doctor's Reality Therapy program on the grounds that the federal government must be going broke. There is no doubt in the minds of the staff of Building 206 that Roy will make this step satisfactorily. There is no doubt in the mind of the building doctor that twenty-three started and twenty-three will make it.

As of April 1964, Roy and twenty-one others in the group had been out of the hospital over six months. The twenty-third member, ready to go with the others but held because of lack of funds, had been out four months. This one group represents a total of over three hundred years of hospitalization.

AN INDEPENDENT CONFIRMATION OF REALITY THERAPY

In November of 1962, several months after the initial presentation of Reality Therapy to the National Conference on Crime and Delinquency, I received a letter from Dr. Willard A. Mainord, a psychologist in the state of Washington. Dr. Mainord wrote that in his work with early admissions to a state mental hospital he had come to almost the same conclusions about therapy that I had discovered working with delinquent girls at Ventura. The pioneer work described below was done at Western State Hospital in Washington. Dr. Mainord is now assistant professor of psychology at the University of Louisville. The following, with minor editing, is a paper describing his work, which may be seen to confirm our contention that Reality Therapy is as effective with early admissions as it is with chronic patients.

A THERAPY[3]

It has been some years now since Eysenck began publishing evidence that psychotherapeutic procedures customarily employed have been ineffective. The usual response has been that there is something wrong with Eysenck, inasmuch as everyone knows that psychotherapy works. If any proof is needed, ask therapists and some of their patients, and it is obvious that therapy works miracles in a strangely leisurely way. And if therapies have occasionally not worked, it has been a matter of unskilled therapists, unmotivated patients, and the untreatability of many diagnostic groups. With these cozy explanations always available, we have continued merrily to train more therapists to carry out the same fruitful procedures and have taught them, in the process, that it is only the naïve and/or foolish who actually expect to modify patient behavior with any marked degree of success in less than years and years of excavating, catharting, transferring, insight seeking, and Freud knows what else.

The variations on the theme are apparently endless. Thus we can find ponderous discussions of the dilutions of transference reactions that will make group therapies ineffective. We have it as a matter of principle that something called intellectual insight is useless, but that emotional insight will transform social slobs into creative geniuses. "Symptomatic" treatment is doomed to failure, and active therapists are frustrated sexual exhibitionists. Untherapized therapists can deal only with their own distorted projections, which will lead their patients into a psychic jungle where no Dr. Livingstone presumes. And heaven help the questioning therapist who dares to doubt the dogma for he will soon learn that his destructive powers as a deviate far exceed his constructive powers as a good union man.

In spite of all this, a few brave souls have been raising some questions. Eysenck[4] (if you will forgive the expression) reports that what results have been rather clearly demonstrated, have had

[3] Mainord, W. A. (1962). "A Therapy," *Research Bulletin,* Mental Health Research Institute, Ft. Steilacoom, Wash., 5, 85–92.

[4] Eysenck, H. (1960). *Behavior Therapy and the Neuroses,* New York: Pergamon Press. (Eysenck has been arguing that the procedures of conventional therapy are ineffective and offers a therapy based on learning theory which he claims is more effective.)

a learning theory basis, and he has published a book expanding this heresy.

. . . Szasz[5] has been arguing that mental patients should not be considered as sick people. Instead, he argues that such patients have developed a style of life that results, quite simply, in problems of living. The behavior that can be observed is problem-solving behavior, but will not be modified significantly unless the deficient style of living is improved. All the implications of this point of view are not immediately obvious, but it does suggest that teaching the patient to believe that he is sick is to encourage him to become a passive recipient of whatever treatment the physician recommends. If the patient chooses to wait until he is "cured," chronic hospital residence might be predicted.

The therapy to be described was set up on the admission wards of Western State Hospital in Fort Steilacoom, Washington. The two wards are differentially populated by, conventionally enough, the usual two sexes. Admission policies are such that all patients between 18 and 65, who are not the victim of some known neurological condition, are sent to these two wards. In the past, the patient was worked up and transferred to some other ward inside of two weeks, if possible. Thus, the staffs of these two wards were not involved in any but the briefest of therapeutic efforts and saw only that problems were presented but never solved. It was hoped that it would help to improve staff morale if treatment programs were set up on the admission wards.

To get a program going, the medical staff was asked to submit names of all new admissions that they felt might be able to benefit from intensive, short-term group psychotherapy. Actual selection of the patients, however, has been accomplished by a weekly staff, which usually consists of the administrative chief of the ward, the chief ward nurse, a social worker (if by chance some social history is known—often not the case with such new patients) and by the author. The selection is primarily made by a short interview in which the patient shows some ability to verbalize, to express willingness to work at getting better, and to dimly accept the idea that responsibility for progress is the patient's. About three of every four referrals reach the group. The chief reason for rejection is an apparent lack of ability to function well enough intellectually to

[5] Szasz, T. S. (1961). *The Myth of Mental Illness,* New York. Paul B. Hoeber, Inc. (Whether or not one agrees with all Szasz says, and I for one do not, I would have to agree completely with what Dr. Mainord quotes here.)

keep up with a vigorous and often abstract group. Average group membership is somewhere between 10 and 12.

The patient learns two things the first day in the group. First, and most important, all administrative decisions will be made in the group with the exception of those things that require medical training to evaluate: drugs, physical complaints, etc. This means that all passes, privileges, jobs, trial visits, and discharges will be accomplished through and in the group. Second, the patient is taught that no group member is ever sick; instead, he is crazy. When the word "crazy" is questioned, it is pointed out that the patient does and has done many crazy things. The word "sick" is treated like a dirty word, and any group member who tries to use this concept is in for a rough time from the rest of the group. Finally, the patient is obliged to commit him or herself to complete honesty with the group, and no reservations to this commitment are acceptable. The patient is "dishonest" if he withholds important information from the group, either about himself or about other group members.

It is emphasized from the beginning that it is not believed that it is necessary to modify the patients' assets so that no group time will be spent in recognizing or in unearthing hidden nobility. Rather, it is suggested that any improvement in emotional tone will result from the identification and improving of methods of behaving which are essentially evasive, irresponsible, and dishonest. Sooner or later the new group member reaches the conclusion that he or she is immoral by his or her own standards, and the group agrees. This makes it possible for the patient to come up with some concrete goals which involve the improvement of behavior in the desired direction whether or not the patient feels ready to do so. Usually some time is spent in getting rid of what we have learned to call the "I'm-too-good-for-this-world" syndrome. The group will never accept noble reasons for bad behavior, and the patient is forced to look at all the obligations and commitments which have been accepted and given and which have not been kept.

Upon entering the group, the patient is required to pay for treatment by taking on some work detail and can earn no privileges until work has become part of the daily schedule. Inasmuch as the group members are the only permanent patients on the ward, they are given the responsibility for seeing that no work is done by the nursing staff that can be legally done by the patients.

Thus they run the kitchen, the clothes room, all housekeeping details, as well as provide clerical help wherever it is then needed in the hospital. Good performance is expected, and ground privileges are withheld if work is not satisfactory.

Group members are given the responsibility of getting off drugs as soon as they can convince their respective physicians that they are capable of functioning without pills. They are also given the responsibility of learning how to get along with staff members even though often the staff member in question may basically be in the wrong. All staff members working with these patients are asked to lean over backwards to avoid any impression that the patient needs to be babied or favored in any way.

Responsibility is thrown at the patient in every possible way. If the patient is married to an alcoholic ne'er-do-well, the group works on how the patient may be making marriage intolerable. If the patient is dominated by a smothering parent, the group digs into the "lack of guts" of the patient. If the patient is visibly and deeply depressed, the group works to find out what are the ways in which the patient has earned and deserves to feel so badly. Any attempt to place responsibility upon anyone who is not a group member is not considered to be acceptable group behavior.

Much time is spent upon the concept of freedom of choice, which seems essential in obtaining motivated patients who will behave in ways that can be reinforced. Thus, the group will never accept the idea that "I can't help myself when I want a drink," etc. It is at such times that the "You're-not-sick, you're crazy" technique seems dramatically useful. Patients can comfortably be sick; but when told they are making crazy choices merely because it is easier that way, they typically respond with vigorous efforts to prove their ability to be responsible.

Historical material is not sought for, although typically much is spontaneously offered and discussed. However, when the patient offers some reason out of the distant past for current feelings of guilt, the group denies the validity of such an explanation and insists upon examining current reasons for guilt which are assumed to be deserved. No group member can get the group to accept the idea that guilt is the result of an over-punitive superego.

It is always assumed that much of the patient's behavior is designed to manipulate others, and the group is constantly alert to such manipulations which are usually in evidence right on the ward and within the group. Bids for sympathy and collections of injustices are brusquely and directly counter-attacked.

Simple learning theory notions are rigidly applied. Behaviors which are sought will be reinforced positively; those which are troublesome are reinforced negatively. Feedback within the group is a constant part of every administrative decision. Often the group is consulted about whether or not the group has evidence that the patient has earned a yes answer to a request, but there is no attempt to pretend that the group is a democratic institution. It is clearly stated that the therapist is the expert in the group and will behave as arbitrarily as he wishes. He makes his pledge to the group that he is going to make decisions for the benefit of the patient no matter what the patient thinks about it.

The therapist deliberately takes a vigorous, directive role and tells the group that they have the job of learning how to handle him. He warns that he plans to be tough enough so that if they can handle him they will be able to handle almost anybody. Silence is not tolerated; this is merely an evasion of responsibility, although interestingly enough silence has never been a problem since the first week of the group's existence. Usually the problem is to find enough time for all the potential participants asking to be heard.

The therapist reserves the right to speak to whomever he chooses, about whatever he chooses, and will respect no confidences unless he feels that some useful purpose would be served. He may bring into the group at any time anything he may have learned from any source—staff members, other patients, friends or relatives. A similar arrangement is maintained—particularly with family members—so that the therapist can speak freely to whomever he encounters. Typically, interviews with relatives are conducted in the presence of the patient although there are many exceptions to this. One of the group rules is that there is nothing that is not appropriate for the group's consideration if it is important to the patient, and the therapist rather than the patient will be the judge of this.

The therapist will allow or actually encourage hostility expressed toward him, but will always deal with it as if the patient is guiltily defensive until it is clear that the therapist was in error, at which point he must say so. However, the patient is also given the responsibility for the nonverbal messages that may be conveyed to others, and this usually resolves the issue. The therapist is not responsible for getting silent group members to participate until the patient has been inactive so long that the accumulated silence can be dealt with as an evasion of responsibility. The therapist will take the responsibility of seeing to it that no patient successfully filibusters either the therapist or the group.

The therapist will use whatever techniques he wishes including humor, scolding, delivering of ultimata, or dismissal from the group. Any patient is free to argue or to question, but it had better be from evidence or logic or this will be seen as irresponsibility. Patient rights are given little consideration; these, too, are to be earned, not bestowed.

This perhaps sounds grim and harsh but in practice the group is more active, engages in more humor, and is more intimately involved in both the group and in therapy than any group seen by the author over an 8-year span. Patient reaction to the therapist is often initially hostile but soon changes to an apparently relaxed yet respectful attitude. The group feels free to express itself with a bit of hostile humor; thus the therapist found in his chair a printed sign advertising his services for five cents.

The first group—on the women's ward—was established in September 1961. On the men's ward, a psychology interne using roughly these same procedures established his group in November and terminated it in early May 1962. Since the groups are treated in the same way and are under—ultimately—the control of the same therapist, the figures to date will be lumped together. As of Friday, August 10, 1962, a total of 125 patients have been admitted to the groups. Twelve were dropped, 8 by their own request and 4 because they appeared untreatable within short-term time limits imposed initially. Fourteen are still members, leaving 100 that have been released from the hospital. Of the 99, seven have returned; 4 of these have again left the hospital, and the others are expected to leave inside of a month. While it is too early to make statistical claims, we would have expected at least 25 returns (conservatively) by this date. Overall, 75 women have graduated, with 3 returns, and 25 men with 4 returns. The average stay in the group of the discharged patients has been slightly over two months. As the groups meet every day for at least an hour and a half, the average graduate has been in therapy for 60 to 70 hours.

The age range of the patients has been from 17 to 59, although the typical patient is in the late twenties or early thirties. Almost all diagnostic categories have been included and, perhaps predictably, depressed patients have been the most rapid to respond. In a surprising number of cases, the prognosis has been considered to be very poor indeed as there has been a weighting towards patients with drinking and drug problems. No standard mental illness diagnostic category has been missed.

We felt a good deal of uneasiness in establishing this program; so it was not surprising to find that many staff members were disturbed at what we were doing. It is probable that the program would have had even more opposition if it were not so obvious that the group members themselves are vigorously pushing its value. Testimonials abound, often from unexpected sources. The best indicator, however, is that the group members talk with new arrivals, and we have far more patients asking for the group than we can possibly accommodate. We are in the process of trying to find a way to establish another group because of the patient response to the program.

It may be wondered what we do about the traditional problems of transference, repressed materials, symptom substitution, etc. The answer is, consciously, nothing. All the materials are there for a more traditional therapy, but we do not look for any particular course of therapy; we merely look for improved behavior which always seems accompanied by improved emotional states. We believe that the consequences of behavior determine emotional tone; so if we can control the behavior, we believe we also control the feeling. We are arguing the so-called symptoms are the illness and if they are given up, therapy is complete.

It should not be concluded that we believe that the apparent success of this therapeutic technique necessarily implies anything about the genesis of emotional disorder. There has never seemed any logical necessity for psychotherapy to be determined by theories of the development of psychopathy. It seems to us that perhaps the chief reason that this approach appeals to the patient is that it gives him hope. If he is sick, he is really quite bewildered as to what he might do about his plight. If, however, he is being irresponsible, evasive, dishonest, and deceitful and if this is causing his emotional pain, it seems obvious to him what he must do; luckily it is something he believes that he can do.

The place of the learning theory procedures should not be minimized; over and over again behaviors are identified, discussed, and then either rewarded or punished. This procedure uses only a small portion of group time, but makes the group influence felt all day, every day, and helps make each entire day part of a therapeutic experience. The group showed its real desire to deal with important problems by scheduling on their own a weekly meeting to take care of problems of ward performance such as dishwashing, bedmaking, etc. Their reason for doing this was that they are unwilling to waste group time discussing these things.

We, of course, are still evolving, still questioning, and still blundering. However, some tentative conclusions can be suggested: patients with much out-patient psychotherapy are going to be extremely difficult to reach in a short period of time; they usually have been successfully taught that they are sick. Patients who have had previous experiences with Electric Shock Treatment and have felt benefited are the most difficult of all group members to reach. Age is less important than expected, although obviously a factor. Women are much easier to treat than men, chiefly it appears because men are much more concerned with saving face. If a mistake is going to be made, it will probably be on the side of asking too little rather than too much of the patient; we have found over and over again that we pay the biggest price whenever we slip on the side of being too undemanding or too accepting of deviant behavior. While it is obvious that therapist personality traits would be important in this type of therapy, the evidence seems to indicate that the approach is teachable. One psychology interne, three R.N.'s, and one nursing assistant have been taught to run the groups adequately although, of course, they are not equally effective.

Finally, we would like to close this paper with a quote from our first group member to leave the hospital. She was pregnant by a man other than her husband, but she had told her husband what had happened, and he was going to work at accepting her back. The family was financially impoverished, the husband working only part time. The patient had just discarded her parents as a source of financial help. She had three children that she would have to take care of, and it was obvious that she would have to work until she delivered. She had several physical ailments, and she had emerged from a black depression engendered by precisely the situation to which she was returning. Her final message to the group was, "It's wonderful to be free."

5 | The Office Practice of Reality Therapy

The cases in this chapter have been selected to illustrate the variety of patients in private practice who can be treated with Reality Therapy. Essential as the principles of involvement, rejection of irresponsibility, and relearning are to the process, there is no static formula for applying them to an individual patient in therapy. How it is done is determined both by the kind of irresponsibility the patient presents and by his personality. Although no two cases are the same, where therapy does succeed one can easily see how these necessary principles were properly interwoven into the treatment process. When the patient fails to gain in responsibility or quits therapy, review of the case almost always shows that the therapist failed to apply properly these same essential principles, cited in detail in Chapter 1.

Difficult as the principles of Reality Therapy may be to apply in practice, now at least I know fairly well what they are. This has not always been the case. Dissatisfied with traditional therapy as early as my last year of training, I was groping for a better way to treat people than what was being taught. It was during this period that a small, unhappy boy was assigned to me for treatment. It was to be many years before I was able to understand why this boy changed so drastically, but if there was a time when Reality Therapy began for me, it was with Aaron.

AARON

Aaron was the highly intelligent eleven-year-old son of an unemotional, overly intellectual divorced woman who worked as a mathematician at one of the Los Angeles missile and space laboratories, and a father who lived in another part of the country and had no contact with him. Aaron was often left home in the care of a neighbor while his mother went away on weekends with her boyfriend. At the time I saw him he had been seen by two other therapists over the previous two years, both third-year residents in a psychiatric training facility. He was assigned to me for treatment when I was also a third-year resident and was my first child outpatient. The other therapists had treated him conventionally with play therapy. Most of their time was spent interpreting the meaning of his play to him. For example, if he struck a female doll repeatedly, the therapist would ask him if he wouldn't like to hit his mother and hope Aaron would confirm the truth of his guess. Having also been trained in traditional psychiatry, I attempted at first to follow in the footsteps of the previous therapists. When Aaron confirmed his anger and hostility against his mother I wondered, as they must have, why this insight did not help him. He wanted to learn better ways to act, but up to then all of us had avoided teaching him what he needed to know.

One way to describe Aaron and his behavior is to say that although he was pleasant in appearance, he was the most obnoxious child I had ever met. I dreaded Monday and Thursday mornings because those days started with Aaron. He evidently had been treated very permissively by his previous therapists who, besides interpreting his behavior to him, accepted everything he did. And what he did was horrible. He ran pell-mell from game to game and toy to toy, never letting me help him to enjoy what he was doing. He seemed to be almost desperately avoiding my offer to play as if my joining in the play might deprive him in some way of some of his pleasures. He acted aggressively in a completely haphazard, unpredictable way, crying for my attention but turning nasty and withdrawing when I gave him some warmth. He discussed his mother in a highly critical way, making her into an ogre of psychiatric rejection. His angry comments paraphrased the words of the previous therapists, especially in his use of adjectives like hostile and rejecting as he described his mother. Criticizing the previous therapists at the clinic in their treatment of him as well as the clinic toys, playrooms, and lack of entertaining facilities, he also rattled on about all the destructive things he did and was planning to do at home.

He blamed his failure to be happy on his mother, her boyfriend, his missing father, or his previous therapists. His school did not escape his critical wrath: it was very bad, his teachers did not understand him, and the other kids picked on him. As time went on, however, he blamed more and more of his predicament upon me. He was preoccupied with his mother's current boyfriend, who had been the subject of voluminous psychiatric interpretations in the past. He had learned to blame many of his problems on the boyfriend, always ending on the martyred note that this man took his mother away from him. A reading of the record showed that his repetitious complaint was almost verbatim from what previous therapists had told him.

Regardless of how he behaved, no one had ever attempted to put a value judgment on his behavior, no one had ever told him he was doing wrong. Everything he did was accepted as something to be explained or, in psychiatric terms, "interpreted" ad nauseum.

Because no one had attempted to set limits for him either in his home or in treatment, he was erratic and unhappy. His behavior was a desperate attempt to force someone to direct his behavior and discipline him so that he might behave better and achieve something worthwhile. All he felt was that no one really cared; he was involved with no one, and lacking the necessary involvement he acted almost totally on impulse.

In his attempt to get someone to set some limits, he tried everything, producing grossly inconsistent behavior. Vocally and physically aggressive at times, he might with equal suddenness become withdrawn and almost detached from reality. He would start a game, then destroy it if he suffered even one minor setback. He walked away from our outdoor play and then would come back to beg me for candy. He would run away, hide, and try to make me look for him all over the clinic. Continually begging for ice cream or for money, he became detached when he was refused. He made it a point never to talk about anything meaningful, that is, what he was doing and feeling. If it came up naturally in conversation he would stop suddenly and run, scream, or begin to talk gibberish. Several times during each session he would tell me that his mother did not like him and that her dislike caused his troubles. It was some time before I began to realize that he was well aware of his behavior, even to the extent that in his own erratic, impulsive way he devised new tests for my patience. He actually planned some of his misconduct, which must have been exhausting and difficult for him to keep up as long as he did.

His mother was an impersonal, detached individual who raised Aaron as an object rather than a person. Instead of reacting to his behavior and setting some limits, she discussed it with him objectively. Essentially a cold woman, she did contribute to his frustration, but if our hope was for her to change, Aaron had little chance. Basically Aaron felt worthless and unloved. From material in the record it was apparent that the school had given up trying to reach this intelligent boy and was just trying to live with him. He made fair grades in subject matter, but he was a disrupting influence in the classroom and in all his social contacts. The other children in school and around his neighborhood shunned him like the plague, precipitating further anger and obnoxious behavior, which in turn caused them to shun him even more. At home or in school he interrupted their play, destroyed their creative attempts, and broke into their recitations in class with snide remarks.

Although Aaron was desperate for some change, I was advised by my supervisor to continue to work with him in play therapy and to interpret his "anal retention and oral aggression." A firm believer in psychoanalytic theory, my supervisor was convinced that the child needed to know "why." Once his behavior was interpreted to him in terms of the transference—that he was reacting to the therapist as a good father and also as a bad abandoning father—he should be able to change. My supervisor also thought that many of Aaron's problems could be solved if his mother, through weekly conferences with a social worker, could gain insight into her role in his difficulties and improve her treatment of him; two years of traditional social work conferences, however, had produced only more intellectualizing from her. My supervisor failed to recognize the desperate, present situation in which Aaron was doing his best to change.

Although it was to be many years before Reality Therapy became definite in my mind as a method of treatment, it was with Aaron that I first discovered the dramatic force of confronting a child with present reality. This confrontation, fortunately made after we had gained some involvement, solidified our relationship into a deeper therapeutic involvement which produced great changes in Aaron.

I realized dimly that in following the principles of orthodox therapy I was contributing to Aaron's present desperation rather than relieving it, and I made up my mind to change my approach. Against all my training and reading, and without telling anyone what I planned to do, I began a kind of Reality Therapy. The explaining was over. From now on we were going to emphasize reality and present behavior.

When Aaron arrived the following morning I took him into my office, nudging him gently past the playroom when he tried to stop there as usual. Telling him to sit down and listen, I explained that I wasn't interested in anything he had to say, only that he listen to me this morning. He whined and tried to get away, but I held him and faced him toward me. I told him to shut up and for once in his life to listen to what someone had to say. I informed him that the play was over, that we would sit and talk in an adult fashion, or if we walked we would walk as adults. I explained clearly that I would not tolerate any running away or even any impolite behavior while we were walking. He would have to be courteous and try to converse with me when I talked to him. He was to tell me everything he did and I would help him decide whether it was right or wrong.

When he immediately attempted to leave, I forcibly restrained him. When he tried to hit me, I told him I would hit him back! After two years without restraint, it was probably the suddenness of this approach that shocked him into going along with me. After some brief initial testing, he did not resist much, probably because he had been anxious for so long to be treated in this realistic way. Also, apparently sensing my own desperation, he was afraid that if he pushed me too far I would leave, and he needed me very much.

I wanted to know what he did in school and at home, and what he could do that was better. When I told him frankly that he was the most miserable and obnoxious child I had ever met, he was greatly surprised. He had thought all therapists must automatically love their patients. I informed him that if he stayed in therapy he was going to have to change because neither I nor anyone else could possibly care for him the way he was now.

What happened next was most dramatic. First of all, he became likable, talking to me courteously. He seemed to enjoy being with me and surprisingly I began to look forward to seeing him. Even though we were now becoming involved, he complained to his mother about my tactics. He knew that she would be upset, and he wanted to find out if she could make me change my new approach to him. If his mother had been able to change me then, it would have proved that I did not really care and our involvement would have been broken. She sought me out as he knew she would, and asked me what I had in mind. When I told her that I was definitely going to continue with my new method, she threatened to take my "unpsychiatric behavior" to my child psychiatry supervisor. I bluffed her by telling her to do so. Had she told him I would have been in trouble, but the bluff worked. Aaron did not complain further and she never took any action against me. I discussed other cases with my supervisor, mentioning Aaron only to say that he was doing much better.

Rapidly Aaron and I grew more involved. Criticizing him for all his old weaknesses but praising him when he did well, I stood in his path whenever he tried to revert to his old ways.

In about six weeks he changed remarkably. I heard from his school that his work had suddenly risen to straight A and that his behavior had also become excellent. The teachers couldn't understand what had happened. I told them to be firm with him, treat him as kindly as they could, and not to make any comments about his changed performance. At home his mother noticed the changes that began to occur there also and, while she liked his new behavior, she was uncomfortable because he was "so different." Having always seen him as some kind of a miserable little boy creature, she found it difficult to relate to him as a responsible boy because of her poor attitude toward men and people in general.

Her atttiude didn't seem to bother Aaron at all. He was only slightly involved with his mother, and he was now getting satisfaction from his relationships with other people. He rather enjoyed his mother's discomfort and her inability to understand what had happened to him. I told her very little other than to treat him as an adult and to expect good behavior. After a while she began to get used to her different son and eventually their relationship became a little better. Theirs will never be a warm, good, mother-son relationship, but it became far better than it had been in the past. As he began to play constructively with other children, for the first time in his life playmates began to seek him out.

About three months later he was discharged from therapy. He had developed a good relationship with his mother's boyfriend, and it was their new relationship which was going to make marriage between his mother and this man possible. Aaron would benefit because he certainly needed a father. After the marriage had been decided on, I thought it was a good time for him to quit therapy. School was almost over, Aaron had made some friends, and he needed me much less. I was able to follow the case for six months and he continued to do well. Not only had Aaron benefited greatly from the therapy, but I had learned the valuable lesson that breaking with teaching and tradition as I had done could be beneficial. I was encouraged to continue in the direction that will be described in the remaining cases in this chapter.

In private practice patients who are fairly responsible except for a particular problem often come for treatment. Unhappy as they and their families may be with the way they are, they usually present no great problem to anyone outside the family. As long as psychiatrists are in private practice, patients who have the means to do so will come looking for what they feel is missing in their lives. Treating them is difficult because the therapist cannot use the firmness or direction that he can employ in institutions or even with some clinic patients such as Aaron. Results come slowly and the gain in responsibility is never as dramatic as in cases in which the therapist has more control.

PAT

A wealthy, young, overindulged, satisfactorily married mother of two whose only obvious problem was overweight, Pat is typical of the fairly responsible patients whom the psychiatrist sees. Extremely pleasant, with an agile, intelligent mind, she was skeptical of psychiatry yet hopeful that perhaps through therapy she might gain more from her life. Notwithstanding her material well-being, she felt that there was much she was missing.

The first part of Reality Therapy with Pat was difficult for both of us as I tried to create involvemnt between us and she tried to understand what I was driving at. Expecting to discuss her childhood, she found it difficult to understand that I was not particularly interested in historical material. Attempting at times to talk about her dreams and unconscious mind, she found me equally uninterested. Restricting the discussion to the present seemed sterile to her because her life was the rather humdrum existence of the rich suburban housewife who had difficulty in filling her days and much more in talking about what she did. Nevertheless we did find much to discuss about the current status of her large, complex family and also about books, plays, movies, and current events. Stimulated to think about what was going on in the world outside of her limited existence, she enjoyed our discussions, but she continually questioned the therapy and the lack of progress toward a better life.

Her favorite diversion was to take me to task for not helping her to reduce. In addition to her own direct comments, she quoted her husband as saying he could not see one apparent benefit from therapy. According to him she was as fat and difficult to live with as ever. To these attacks on my therapeutic skill I would answer that psychotherapy does not reduce people, that it does not make them happier, and it does not solve their problems. If she wanted to reduce, she was free to do so and I would encourage her, but weight reduction was not my responsibility. I emphasized that if she wanted to change she had to come regularly because I knew that we had to become involved before anything could happen. I did not care what she talked about as long as it had to do with the present. I had to stress both that she must come and that I could do little directly for her because I did not want her to become involved with me as a dependent. Without magic to help her, I would stay with her until the problems she came for were solved. As with every patient, I let her know that I was there as a person who would not desert her or give her false hope.

Discussing her rather irresponsible existence in which she did everything to please herself only, Pat seemed to revel in the long descriptions of her childish behavior toward her husband, her family, and even some of her friends. It was very important to her to tell me how much better she would be if she could act in a more mature way, but how she absolutely would not do so. She was anxious for me to tell her to do something different, which I was tempted to do, but I refrained because I knew she was trying to cast me in the role of reformer so that she could reject me as she had rejected everyone else who had tried to correct her.

Therapy continued slowly, little seemed to be happening, yet the relationship was growing. Unable to make me assume a role she could reject, she began to develop some respect and trust for me and what I was doing. Although she started to come late in an effort to show how little she cared, she did come. I paid no attention to her lateness, or to her insincere apologies or excuses. Finally, one day during a rather innocuous conversation she burst out and said, "There's nothing you can do to make me responsible." Here was a remarkable statement because I had never mention the word responsibility to her. Nevertheless the months of subtle pressure had had their effect. She was now very slightly on the defensive because she was beginning to understand what I was trying to do. I must have been making some headway or this conversation would not have taken place. I was able to increase the pressure on her to change by discussing my work with the delinquent girls. When I pointed out how similar she was to these girls, she readily agreed, saying, "If you help them so much why can't you help me?" To this little pleasantry I replied, "Because I can't lock you up. If I could, you know as well as I do that you would change." Not denying my claim, she countered by stating that all I had was these two hours a week in the office and that's all I ever would have. Since I had no control it was up to her. I added, "I'll wait, I have all the time in the world."

Next Pat attacked my fees by saying that they were too low, another depreciation of my worth. She said she could afford more, other psychiatrists were getting larger fees, why didn't I ask more. I answered her charge by asking if therapy had helped her. When she replied that it hadn't, I said that considering my ineffectiveness

I could hardly charge more, I wasn't worth it. Having thus passed the test of avarice, I was not again challenged on my fees. Through this gambit and countless others we became more deeply involved. She tried everything to prove me irresponsible. I responded by admitting any apparent shortcomings but never giving up. All her efforts were really directed toward having me commit one of two fatal errors—giving up or giving in. Either one would have finished therapy.

After almost a year, we began to be more involved; I could point out her irresponsibilities. My regular presence and my stand for greater responsibility encouraged her to take a chance and change. During the whole of the second year she slowly became more responsible. Although the change was not dramatic, she was less self-centered and more able to give to others, especially to her husband and children, who needed her far more than she was originally able to admit to herself. She felt a keener sense of achievement and she lost fifty pounds. She tried to credit me with the weight loss, but as I refused to take the blame for her inability to lose earlier, I refused to take the credit then.

It was a difficult though rewarding case. With her intelligence and energy, Pat certainly had great capacity for more worthwhile behavior within her immediate surroundings, and perhaps she will have a chance to do more in the larger world. In the final part of therapy we were both groping toward the goal of even greater responsibility.

DEE

Whereas Pat is representative of moderately responsible patients who must be given a minimum of direction, most patients present far more serious problems. For example, at age twenty-five Dee was a promiscuous girl who had borne two illegitimate children, whom she gave up for adoption, and had had several abortions. Willing to sleep with anyone who asked her, she was living with a man for whom she did not care when she came for therapy. It was extremely difficult to get involved with Dee.

Referred to the clinic by a friend who convinced her that she should at least try therapy, she came dressed in shorts and a tee shirt, hardly proper clothes for the university clinic. By means that varied from excessive descriptions of her promiscuous life to her inappropriate dress, she immediately conveyed to me her negative attitude toward therapy and her opinion that little could be done. Neither commenting on her appearance nor becoming interested in her lurid stories, I arranged to see her three hours a week. Trying to concentrate on what she was presently doing, I did not discuss her inappropriate dress until she finally brought up the subject herself. Then I told her that how she dressed was up to her, that she was able to decide how she wanted to look. I added that her raising the subject showed that it must be important to her and that she might think about what she was doing.

It should be mentioned here that Dee was seen concurrently with Aaron and that I was not nearly as comfortable then with what I was doing as I am now. My adult psychiatry supervisor, interested in this case which seemed to him to be refractory to the conventional approach, generally advised me along the lines of Reality Therapy. He was a learned and flexible older psychiatrist who felt that Dee's life seemed so hopeless that a different approach was warranted.

For the whole year in the clinic it was a constant battle between us as she tried to prove to me that any change in her way of life was impossible and I tried to hang on and to become involved with her for the good qualities she had, her good mind, her interest in education, and her basically warm feeling for people, all of which were almost completely obscured by her constant irresponsible behavior.

The most encouraging part of the case was that she came regularly for her appointments. She came late, she dressed poorly—less so as time went on—but she did come. As the year in the clinic approached an end she had to make the choice of going ahead toward living a responsible life or returning to her old ways. She knew that she would no longer be able to see me regularly, but our involvement, which had gathered strength over the year, was now strong enough so that she was able, through phone conversations, letters, occasional visits and very brief periods of private therapy, to start to lead a more satisfying life. Further regular therapy would have straightened her subsequent erratic course but, except for one short period, she never returned to her old ways. When I confronted her with reality at the end of the clinic year, she was involved enough and strong enough to accept it; the previous year had set the stage for the last critical interviews.

Her relationship with me was the first meaningful involvement she had ever had. She tested it to the limit, but she was unsuccessful in getting me to change my appraisal that she is capable of achieving both a better standard of behavior and high educational goals. It is now eight years since she first came to the clinic. No longer vainly attempting to fulfill her need for love through sex, which served to destroy any chance she had to feel worthwhile, she has gained a sense of worth through finishing high school and junior college. Having entered the University of California on a scholarship, she is now preparing to teach in junior college. When she graduates with her bachelor's degree, no one will recognize her as the irresponsible girl who walked into the clinic eight years before.

We continue to keep in touch on an as-needed basis (three or four times a year), but generally she is on her own. Our involvement is such that short phone conversations or an occasional visit help her to overcome tendencies to return to irresponsible patterns. Most of our present discussions center around the things she has to learn to make the most of her education. As in the case of Pat there were no external controls; it was the involvement and the satisfaction gained through responsible behavior which brought Dee this far.

DAN

Dan exemplifies a group of young people who are really ready to face reality but need a small amount of intense therapy to get them started. It is as important to avoid holding them back as it is to urge them ahead. When Dan came to me after several years of traditional therapy with a psychologist, he stated that he came to a psychiatrist to delve deeper into a complex, previously incestuous relationship with his mother coupled with, in his words, "a strong tendency toward latent homosexuality." Impressed by his basically responsible attitudes, I felt that what he most needed was just the opposite of the "deep therapy" he was requesting. I refused to discuss his past, his dreams, and his relationship with his mother.

He said he came to me to find himself, to decide, no matter how long it took, what he should be. Refusing also to talk about this subject, I told him repeatedly to go to work.

Basically Dan was able to fulfill his needs. He was willing to work, he was honest, he liked people, and he seemed capable of giving and receiving love. What he needed was someone to recognize his abilities and then, in a sense, to tell him to "fly right." My quick, direct, honest approach was new to this overly intellectual young man who thought he should search for the meaning of his life before committing himself to go to work. Because I was able to fill the role of the strong male he needed, we became involved in about three sessions. He then went to work and the need to discuss his past failures disappeared.

Altogether I saw Dan no more than a dozen times. He is now working steadily and preparing for a career in art and music during his spare time. His ceramics have been praised and, even more noteworthy, they have been bought. Now out in the real world fulfilling his needs, not sitting idly by, wondering what life is about, he feels worthwhile because he is no longer dependent upon anyone as he pursues his career. He is surprised at how well he gets along with his mother now that he treats her as a mother instead of a forbidden sexual object, and several good relationships with warm, loving girls have put a stop to his worries about homosexuality. Therapy is essentially ended. I hear from him about every three months and I am pleased with his progress. As he gains more success we will lose contact, but when problems arise he can turn to me for constructive direction and encouragement. His knowledge that I will never allow him to evade reality will maintain our involvement as long as necessary.

Some patients who come for therapy are recognized as potentially harmful to themselves and others so that hospitalization is an immediate consideration. They may be mildly psychotic or deeply depressed, yet they are functioning in the world well enough to be able to work. Despite the pressure to play it safe and put them in a hospital, there is one overruling condition which prevents this step. Whereas putting such patients in a hospital tells them that I believe they can't cope with the world, avoiding hospitalization encourages them to put forth the extra effort which may pull them through. Another disadvantage of hospitalization is that removing a patient from his job prevents him from supporting his family, causing additional stress and intensifying his troubles.

Sometimes working with irrational interviews and wild phone calls that include direct threats of suicide and homicide, the therapist makes every effort to bring the relationship to the point where reality can be accepted by the patient. If the therapist is able to withstand the pressure of patients so irresponsible that they may be a danger to themselves or the community, they can be dramatically changed. A recent Christmas card from Jim reminded me of how much he had changed over a three-year period.

JIM

Jim, a highly intelligent electronics engineer, came because he was depressed. Working at a good job, with a wife and two children whom he loved, he felt that he could not face another day. Things were barely real to him, every movement was an effort; he just wanted to stop functioning completely. Hospitalization would have been detrimental to his already sagging morale. Several previous periods of hospitalization with electric shock treatments had provided temporary respite, but now the depression was back in full force and he was looking for more lasting relief. I was also encouraged not to hospitalize him because he had never had any psychotherapy when he was functioning well, although he had been under psychiatric treatment during his depressed periods.

In the first interview I told him both that the depression would pass (he knew it would also, but this was little consolation) and that if he wanted a more permanent solution he should stay in treatment until I discharged him. I emphasized that my goal was higher than helping him through this episode; my goal was to see him until he gained enough strength to overcome the increasing periods of depression that were ruining his life.

In recent years he had become severely depressed every four to six months. I told him to come in every week, that our scheduled hour was essential, and to keep working. I also told him to call me any time, to come in more often if necessary, and that together we would make it day by day, week by week. I gave him one final instruction—and this is the corect word because he was in a numb depression where he needed concrete and forceful direction—he must go to work every day and, if he could do nothing more, at least sit at his desk eight hours no matter how excruciating it became. Probably this last order pulled him through the week that followed. He also began to understand that his present treatment was going to be different from his previous hospitalization and electric shock therapy.

The weeks that followed were nightmarish; he could barely get along. He had no energy, no desire even to eat. He wanted to fade into oblivion. He felt that no one could possibly respect him, that he was of no value to himself or anyone else. Driving became difficult; sitting at his desk was an ordeal. He could do almost no work, but fortunately he was ahead in his project so he could coast awhile. I told him to tell his group leader about his problem and that he was seeing me. Fortunately, this man was compassionate, having had a stomach ulcer for which he too had received psychiatric care. The group leader called me and I told him to be tough and demanding outwardly yet understanding of Jim's temporary inability to do much work. *It is important that depressed patients do not get sympathy because sympathy emphasizes their worthlessness and depresses them even more.*

We continued to struggle along and the depression finally lifted. As it did he was able to describe his real problem. In his depressed state all he had been able to say was that he was wrong and the rest of the world was right. As the depression lifted, however, he was able to describe a serious marriage problem that initially he had not been able to mention. According to what his wife told him, his marriage was failing because he was not able to act enough like a man for her satisfaction. Although his soft, passive demeanor lent some credence to her accusation, his wife had serious problems of her own which she projected onto Jim. When, trying to help the marriage, I asked her to come in, all she could tell me was that she wanted a man just like him, but not him. For her, he was too kind, too soft, too good, and completely unsatisfactory sexually. She was convinced that nothing could help him become the man she wanted. During this time he began, with my help, to get tougher and more masculine. Feeling better for a while, he changed to a new job and hoped his new attitude might save the marriage. When his wife insisted upon a divorce, he again became depressed, blaming his wife's rejection entirely upon himself.

Now, besides having to live alone, he was assigned to a new project for which he had sole responsibility. In the past the group carried him when he became depressed, but now even this crutch was removed. Things looked so black to him that I feared he would kill himself. Fortunately, we had the experience of living through the previous episode together, and we had intensified a warm, firm involvement during the five months between depressions. Because of the involvement I was able to be hard on him as he became depressed. I told him to stop feeling sorry for himself, to go fishing, to go out with girls, and to work voluntarily on weekends to make up for his slowness during the week.

The suggestion that he owed the company something for his inefficiency struck home. Although he always claimed that he did, the possibility of doing something about it had never really occurred to him. I hammered away at how his depression removed him from responsibility. The first good sign occurred when he began to respond to my pressure with anger. I became tougher, he became more angry, and as the anger drained, his depression lifted. I should also add that during the severe phases of the depression I gave him a small dose of a mild stimulant which I feel had more of a psychological than a pharmacological effect.

As he got over the depression a fortunate and to us, looking for some relief from the tension of the preceding months, somewhat humorous event occurred. When Jim gets over depressions he usually feels very good, almost a little euphoric. He was soon able to triple his output at work, almost singlehandedly pushing a critical project to completion. Because the company had only known him when he was mildly or severely depressed his increased work output as the depression lifted resulted in two promotions and three raises in less than four months. We could not help laughing about this fortuitous combination of circumstances.

Therapy continued for a year until we passed two more periods when he ordinarily would have become depressed. He dated and married a woman who not only loves him but also pushes him, something he needs very much. Her attitude is very different from that of his first wife, who criticized him but did not feel he could change, so she did not push him. Interpreting this push as love and interest in him, which it is, he is happier than ever. "Helen now can take over your job," he said in his last Christmas card, which added, "I thought you would like to know that things are going well for Helen and me. She has really been cracking the whip and I think she has me just about straightened out. . . ."

Finally, I would like to describe a patient I am treating now who I anticipate will be in treatment for a long time. Of all the male patients that come for therapy, those with sexual deviations are the most refractory to treat. Regardless of how they manifest their problem—peeping Tom, exhibitionist, fetishist, transvestite, or homosexual—they do not feel themselves to be the sex that nature has given them. Although the mirror may show them to be male, much inside their minds is in disagreement with their reflection. Because of a particular combination of circumstances in their previous life, most of them choose the homosexual role in an effort to fulfill their needs in the best way they can. They have an added obstacle to gaining a real feeling of self-worth or love because their life is based on a biologically false premise. Some try to force themselves into an acceptance of their true role by marrying and having a family. When this fails, as it does in many instances, they become demoralized, caught between their homosexuality and their own well-intentioned but unsuccessful attempts to be heterosexual. I must emphasize here that not all homosexuals are unhappy; those who are satisfied with their role find success in fulfilling their needs, but those who come for therapy never do. Depending upon their circumstances and the strength of the conflict between the life they would like to lead and that which they know they should lead, they may come to a psychiatrist for treatment.

In treatment homosexuals wish to find relief from the misery of the conflict; they want to resolve the problem in one direction or another. The psychiatrist, however, must not fall into the trap of helping them become better adjusted homosexuals, as many patients initially desire, but work in the opposite direction, helping them accept themselves as men so that they can gain a male identity and thereby find love and self-worth in their proper role. To accomplish his task the therapist must, in a relatively short time, perhaps as little as an hour a week, gain a relationship with his homosexual patients in which they feel they are relating to a man as a man. Their basic lack is such a relationship, something which they did not have with their father or any other man in their previous life, and which they must have now if they are to resolve their conflict in the right direction. The therapist cannot be their father or any shadowy transference figure; he must be a strong man who is willing to accept the patient as a man.

FRED

An example of the problems of both the patient and the therapist in the treatment of the homosexual is given by the case of Fred. Desperate to get help because he was caught in a frustrating position between his homosexual desires and his responsibilities toward his wife and family, Fred hoped to resolve the problem somehow. He said honestly that, feeling as he did much of the time, he would like to give up both his family and his respected business position and lead a totally homosexual existence. He had not done so because he knew it would ruin his career, hurt his wife who loves him very much, and have a disastrous effect on his growing children. His marriage was his last attempt to force himself into leading a normal heterosexual existence. Although he loved his wife and children, he felt increasing anxiety when he had to play the male role for long periods unrelieved by homosexual contact. Most of all, he said, he would like to be a woman, have a man take care of him, and change an existence which he feels is a fraud.

From the beginning I laid my cards openly on the table. I told him, as he already knew, that his kind of case was very difficult to treat. If he came, he must understand some conditions of treatment. He was told that he was to come once a week indefinitely; as an added emphasis I added, in a half-serious, half-joking way, that he might have to come for the rest of his life. In stressing the time, the all-important point was made that I would not give up on him. No matter how difficult treatment became, I would stick with him.

The final condition was that I did not want Fred to dwell on his problem during the therapy hour. No matter how much he told me about his homosexual feelings, I had no magic words to banish homosexuality. I was willing to discuss anything else. Heterosexuality was fine, as well as business, jokes, books, movies, the world situation, politics, and sports. Only in a crisis, such as his wanting to leave his work and family, would we discuss his problem, and then only to arrive at some way in which he could gain temporary relief. I credited him with being the expert on homosexuality because he had read almost every reputable book on the subject.

In addition to homosexuality—his childhood, his traumas, and his deprivations were also subjects I did not want to hear about. He confirmed the fact that his two previous therapists had been through these conventional areas of discussion; his childhood, for example, had been combed with a fine-tooth comb. Even so, six months after therapy began he caught me off guard and told me of the summer when he was seventeen when he had had intercourse several times with his mother. To this I responded, "So what, is this what makes you queer today?" The disclosure, very dramatic in his mind and designed to shock me, occurred after a critical therapy hour in which he described his desire to break up his home again. It was his way of testing me, trying to find out if I really could care for a person who had committed incest, and my brusque, joking answer came as a great relief to him. Rather than harming our relationship, my response made it stronger. I was not accepting any reason, even this very dramatic one, for him to be the way he was.

He made spectacular progress at activities not related to sex. During the first year I saw him he climbed the executive ladder to an extremely responsible position for his age. Everything he seems to turn to, except for his particular problem, becomes a great success. Therapy with Fred goes on and on. Never complaining at our slow progress, he comes faithfully as we are becoming more involved. Recently he told me of a sexual urge for a married woman with whom he had once had a brief affair, which encouraged me in my belief that he can eventually lead a heterosexual life. I did not discourage his pursuit of this woman even though it is morally unsound. Rather, I kidded with him, saying, "What the hell kind of a queer are you turning out to be? You better watch your step or I'll throw you out of therapy."

To be able to provoke genuine laughter with this remark proved the gathering strength of our involvement. We now have enough involvement so that during a crisis, when he wants to run away into the homosexual world, I can coldly confront him with his responsibility to his children, which wrenches him emotionally and serves to prevent him from giving up. Even though it may seem cruel to put Fred through such an emotional ordeal, there is no other choice; if I did not do so, he would lose respect for me. In years to come I hope to be able to report a successful conclusion to this case that so vitally affects the future of a family.

The cases in this chapter illustrate the use of Reality Therapy with patients who come to the psychiatrist's office. No attempt has been made to describe the intimate details of therapy because no book can do so. Although each case presents a different problem, they are all approached through the use of the principles described in Chapter 1.

When therapy seems finished there is often a problem of when and how to bring it to a close. Although termination is always difficult because of the involvement, as the patient grows stronger he is able to make more permanent involvements to replace the therapist. The therapist must take the initiative if the patient hesitates, but usually termination just happens. To quote Dr. Harrington when I asked him when he believes a patient is ready to have therapy terminated, "When, after a long period of treatment, he begins to talk about how much more he needs a new car and how much less he needs you."

6 | The Application of Reality Therapy to the Public Schools— Mental Hygiene

The success of Building 206 and the Ventura School depends upon the ability of the staff to learn to use the principles of Reality Therapy. In our work at these institutions, both Dr. Harrington and I consider ourselves to be teachers even more than therapists. We have been gratified by the way in which the principles of Reality Therapy have been learned and put into practice by people who have little or no formal training in the social sciences, but who do have a desire to become personally involved with patients. Both institutions house highly irresponsible people who have already suffered a great deal themselves and who almost always have caused others to suffer as well. Years of their lives have been wasted by their failure to learn to fulfill their needs.

Unfortunately, under our present system there is no provision for helping people before they manifest serious irresponsibility. Increasing numbers of mental hospitals, correctional institutions, and psychiatric facilities are required because so many people have not been taught to fulfill their needs early in their lives. Planned programs for mental hygiene (the commonly accepted term for the prevention of irresponsibility) directed toward teaching children to fulfill their needs so that they do not need psychiatric treatment later in life are essentially nonexistent. Our departments of mental hygiene are really departments of psychiatric custody with varying degrees of treatment. True mental hygiene has not proceeded past the discussion phase in most states, in many not even that far.

It is my belief that mental hygiene is stalled because our present psychiatric approach emphasizes mental illness rather than responsibility. The public schools, by far the most logical place to do any real preventive psychiatry, are reluctant to associate themselves with any program so completely identified with the "mentally ill." Until we can rid ourselves of the idea of mental illness and the concept that people who need psychiatric treatment are "sick," we will never be able to enlist public support for a mental hygiene program in the public schools. Assuming, however, that the emotional obstacle of "mental illness" could be overcome and that the schools were willing to participate in a mental hygiene program, conventional psychiatric concepts would be totally inadequate for the job. As long as we cling to the belief that to help problem children we need highly trained professional people working in the traditional areas of case history, unconscious conflicts, insight, and transference, there will be no way to approach the public schools. As shown in Chapters 3 and 4, these concepts are not applicable even to large mental hospitals and correctional institutions because realistically almost all of the treatment is necessarily done by nonprofessional people such as aides and counselors.

We believe that in contrast to conventional psychiatry, Reality Therapy, which has been successfully taught and used on patients in Building 206 and at Ventura, could be applied in the public schools with good results. In a very limited way, Reality Therapy is now being used successfully in the schools in Los Angeles, San Diego, and Sacramento, California.

For the past three years, the last two at U.C.L.A., I have given a one-semester course teaching the principles of Reality Therapy to interested school teachers. The course is aimed directly at helping them work more effectively with irresponsible children in their classes. The teachers, who come from elementary schools and junior and senior highs, with a sprinkling of school counselors, school nurses, and nursery school teachers, have proved to be interested and apt students, all of whom testify that they have no shortage of irresponsible children in their classes. They have been trying to find better ways to cope with students whose wide varieties of misbehavior interfere with their own education and the education of others in the class. By the end of the semester the teachers, with few exceptions, are able to do a significantly better job than they were doing before in helping the problem children in their classes improve their behavior and usually also their school work.

The class meets for two and one-half hours one evening a week for fifteen weeks. During the first one and one-half hours of each class period my lectures describe in detail how responsible people function, how they became the way they are, and, near the end of the semester, the proper treatment of irresponsible people. The final hour of the class period consists of case presentations by the teachers of problem children in their own classes. The purpose of these presentations is to discover in what ways the child is not fulfilling his needs and then to work out a plan through which the teacher, either in class or, in a few cases, with the aid of other teachers in the school, can help the child to fulfill his needs.

Once the child begins to fulfill his needs, his behavior improves greatly, he learns much more easily, and he becomes generally a more responsible person. Only rarely are parents, who are often much more difficult to work with than are the children, included in these plans; the stress is on what the teacher at the school can do. As in the work at Ventura, the emphasis is to help the child toward better behavior which in itself may do much to correct a bad situation that exists at home.

Emphasizing that few of their problems with their students are insoluble if the proper approach can be worked out, I encourage free discussion during the class and follow informal, friendly procedures to stimulate thinking and expression of ideas. Much time is spent explaining how children behave, both to increase the teachers' understanding and to fortify them against lapsing into their previous belief that the child's behavior is indicative of a deep-seated illness.

It takes a long time to give up ingrained beliefs about mental illness and to learn instead that the child's behavior is the best way that he has discovered to fulfill his needs. To accomplish the relearning, I have found it necessary to go through many varieties of irresponsible behavior, not to make diagnoses, but to help the teacher become familiar and comfortable with any kind of problem a child might present. They must learn that a child who is withdrawn and talks to himself in class acts that way because he cannot fulfill his needs. The teacher need not become frantic with the fear that she has a mentally ill child on her psychiatrically unprofessional hands. Instead, she can react with kindness, try to get involved with him, point out his behavior, and get him to do something worthwhile in class. The child who is already seriously withdrawn desperately needs this approach. Finding his teacher unafraid and accepting him although not accepting his behavior, he may change because of the warm, human contact the teacher is able to establish.

By the end of the course, when the more formal lectures on Reality Therapy are given, the teachers already know from the earlier lectures, discussions, and the extensive case presentations approximately what I am going to say. Reality Therapy then comes as a natural outgrowth to what has been learned all semester. The teachers have no trouble understanding that they must become involved with a child, reject his irresponsible behavior, and then teach him better ways to behave. Most of them find themselves already using Reality Therapy, and many have commented that they do not seem to have the difficulty that they once had in dealing with problem students.

In teaching the course I must develop an involvement with the students similar to a therapeutic involvement. The homework is primarily trying to apply in their classes what they learn in the course. In addition, there are short assignments of reading in the text.[1] Grades are not important; learning is measured by the ability not to repeat my words but to put the concepts being taught into action. These abilities are not necessarily related. The teachers must feel that the class is a personal rather than a pedagogical experience, that I am involved with them, that I deeply believe that they can use what I teach, and that I am trying to the best of my ability to show them better ways. They must learn to reject their

[1] Glasser, William, *Mental Health or Mental Illness?* New York: Harper & Brothers, 1961.

previous, inadequate ideas based on the concept of mental illness, give up their reluctance to work with problem children, and accept the idea that the classroom is the best place to do it. Suspending a child from school, necessary as it may sometimes be to allow the school to continue to function, never helps the child.

The teachers develop a new confidence in their own ability to understand their children. They learn new techniques to help children fulfill their needs, techniques which always require them to give of themselves and become more involved with their students. At the same time they learn the necessity of enforcing firm discipline, never in a punitive sense, but to show that they care about their students. The importance of personal contact in teaching has been receiving less attention in recent years as the emphasis on methods, objective testing, and classification of students has increased. Unfortunately teachers have been trained (partly as a carry-over from conventional psychiatry) not to get involved with students, but to remain objective and detached. In contrast I teach and try to show by example that teaching should be a very personal experience for the student. For instance, the teacher should always say, "I want you to . . .", never "we should . . ." or "you should . . ." when giving a child directions. A child's ability to live a successful life depends upon a series of personal involvements with responsible people, and teachers are among the most important people a child encounters.

Reality Therapy emphasizes that closeness is necessary to help a person fulfill his needs so that no teacher need be afraid of closeness. It is almost certain that a teacher who develops a close relationship with a problem child is giving the child the first warm, human involvement he has experienced in a long time. If the child is not sufficiently involved, he will not learn to fulfill his needs, leading to more expressions of his particular kind of irresponsible behavior. We must reject the idea that it is good to be objective with people; objectivity is good only when working with their irresponsible behavior. Treating children as objects rather than as people who desperately need involvement to fulfill their needs only compounds the problem.

When I first present my ideas to a school audience, the initial reaction is often that although the ideas may be sound for Ventura

School where time is ample, they will take too much time to implement for the hard-pressed public school teacher. The teachers are anxious to help students, but they feel that they do not have the time to get involved. My answer is that they do not have the time not to get involved. It takes less of a teacher's time to give the child the personal human touch coupled with firm disciplinary limits that will lead to change rather than to struggle endlessly to discipline a child with whom the teacher has no contact. With young children, or with older but moderately irresponsible children still in the public schools, involvement can occur in minutes, sometimes in seconds.

The first class that I taught included a teacher who worked with the mentally retarded in a high school industrial arts class. Part of his job was to teach the boys the proper use of simple tools. Disturbed because one large boy threatened others with the tools and was aggressive toward everyone, the teacher attempted to handle the boy by not allowing him to use any tools and by lecturing him when he was abusive to other students.

Although he presented the case because the boy caused him so much trouble and took so much of his time, he did not fully realize how much time and energy this boy really was draining from his teaching effectiveness. Because the lectures and the restrictions were ineffective, he was trying unsuccessfully to have the boy removed from the class. He blamed his principal, who he said was unreasonable because he would not transfer the boy.

In the class discussion he did admit that there was no good place to which this large, abusive boy (who also had epileptic seizures) could be transferred, and that suspending him from school to roam the neighborhood as an outcast was no solution. Without admitting how much time he was spending with the boy, he doggedly stated he had no time to do any personal counseling with any student because he was far too busy. He had the unfortunate "show me" attitude of the frustrated teacher who tries to solve a problem by removing it.

I asked him if he could devote ten seconds twice a day to the boy to start a program, a request so limited that he could not refuse. I suggested that he put his arm around the boy's shoulder each day when he entered and when he left class, saying that he was glad to have the boy in class and asking whether he could help him to do the work. It should be made clear that a mentally retarded boy such as this would appreciate the new approach rather than be suspicious of the teacher's change in attitude. Following my suggestion for one week, the teacher reported a remarkable change. The boy was pleasant, and his aggressive, abusive behavior had almost stopped. A total investment of about two minutes had started the involvement and had begun the behavior change.

Next it was necessary to help the boy increase his self-worth or the involvement would not be maintained. The class suggested that the teacher, who would still not allow the boy to use the large or sharp tools, might make him custodian of a few garden tools after the other children put them down and were safely away. The teacher was to check the boy's work in cleaning the tools and putting them away properly and give him praise if it was warranted.

This approach also worked well. Each week in our class we suggested ways that the teacher could increase the boy's scope in the shop class and each week the boy responded as he and the teacher became increasingly involved. His behavior became better in all his other classes as well. The principal took note of the change by praising the teacher for the help he was giving the boy. Graduated with the limited diploma given to the older retarded students, the boy was potentially employable in a menial job. Because of the boy, this example cannot be called typical; nevertheless it illustrates how the principles of Reality Therapy can be applied in the classroom and that they take less of the teachers' time than their old methods.

When he presented the case, the teacher was confused and frightened by the boy who was causing him so much trouble. When the teacher gained the confidence to change his own attitude and behavior, the boy changed. In their relationship something personal was required from the teacher. Had he merely changed his behavior little would have happened.

Over the past six semesters there has been a series of similar cases. Each time the teacher had to become involved, to reject the irresponsibility, and to teach the child better ways. Because few cases are as clean-cut as the previous one, the teacher must often use a variety of techniques, trying one after another until he strikes the right one. Many times it appears that it is the teacher's persistence and the attitude change which reaches the child. Children who are irresponsible ordinarily distrust the teacher, reject his attempt to be personal, and often test him to the limit. The teacher must learn to keep a consistent attitude while varying his approach, and never giving up.

Recently we had a teacher present a first-grade child who was wild, disorderly, and belligerent. The class suggested putting the necessary constant discipline on a personal level. She did so and reported poor results; in fact, the boy seemed to be worse. She was told to keep it up despite the poor results, not to remind him of his past failures, and to start each day with the personal requests such as, "I want you to stay in line," or, "It is important to me that you sit in your seat in class," as if she were using them for the first time. Probably without the encouragement of the class she would have stopped. After about two months the six-year-old started to respond slowly and steadily. By mid-semester he was no problem, and other teachers who observed him in the playground remarked on his improved behavior. Although the consistent approach helped, it was the personal touch that caused the change.

ANDREA

The following example illustrates the startling results that can be obtained by varying the standard classroom approach. Andrea is an attractive and pampered fourteen-year-old girl from a well-to-do home who saw no reason to apply herself in school. Possessing good intelligence, she was pleasant and personable, but she did no work. She had been placed in a special class with others like herself who were not able to accomplish the minimum requirements of regular classes. Because Andrea was clearly capable of doing good work, the teacher had tried, and failed, to reach her with extra attention coupled with personal requests for more work. Although her class work was reasonably good for the special class, she did absolutely no homework.

After a long discussion in our class, it was suggested that the teacher completely stop grading the girl's papers. On the next fairly good class assignment, she was to write *Thank you* at the top of the paper instead of a grade. She had the opportunity to do so almost immediately. When Andrea got her paper back, she stayed after class to ask what was going on. The teacher had been instructed to say nothing of grades, remarking only, "It was a good paper, I appreciated it, and I am letting you know." The girl walked out puzzled but interested. The teacher had reached her; she felt special in some way, different from any feeling she had had in the past.

Thereafter, instead of a grade, all papers received a personal comment such as, "I appreciate your good work," "An interesting opinion," "It's possible you overlooked some points but good work," etc. Any pertinent comment that was primarily complimentary could have been used. The change in Andrea was marked. After just three weeks her work, which now included all the homework assignments, reached A level and stayed there.

Several weeks ago Andrea asked the teacher for a grade on the excuse that her parents wanted to know how she was doing. The teacher told her to put any grade on the paper she thought it deserved and that she would sign it. Interestingly, she put a C on the paper, which was worth at least a B+. The teacher signed it and said nothing. Andrea reported her parents were very satisfied with the C, a great improvement over her previous work. When she returned the paper she said that she felt she was doing better and would give herself a B next time. Not only is she continuing to do well scholastically, she has become an unasked assistant to the teacher, quieting the class and getting them to work even before the teacher arrives.

Few stories are as dramatic as this example which shows that when children who are not seriously irresponsible are able to gain involvement, which usually is not difficult, they are able to improve their work with little further effort from the teacher. Once involvement is attained, the nature of the class situation takes care of the rejection of the irresponsibility and the relearning phases of therapy. The trick is to get involved, and this case demonstrates how easily it can be done if the right key can be found.

ELLEN

Of the many techniques for gaining involvement, one appears to be particularly effective with small children. According to the teachers who have used it, it is fun for the whole class. To illustrate, let me present the case of Ellen, a seven-year-old girl who was an extremely difficult problem in her elementary room class because she stole from everyone. She took things both from the teachers and from the other children; nothing of value was safe in the class. Besides stealing, she had temper tantrums, ran out of the room when frustrated, and demanded excessive attention and affection from her teachers.

At her wit's end when she presented Ellen to our class, the teacher was desperate for some approach that could reach Ellen. Although the teacher emphasized that her home situation was bad, we did not devote time to it because it was unlikely that we could change it. Our job was to work with the child in class to teach her more responsible ways. It was obvious to everyone that she was stealing to try to get attention, apparently to make up for the warmth and affection which she was missing at home.

Stealing is an illogical substitute for a warm relationship, but it was the best she could do to gain the recognition that she desperately needed. Gaining involvement presented a difficult problem. It was obvious that she was involved to some extent with the teacher because most of her stealing was from her, but she was not involved enough for the teacher to be able to help her stop her irresponsible behavior.

Our initial problem was to help the teacher become more involved with Ellen so that she could use the involvement as a start to establishing a better pattern of behavior. In the class discussion some suggested that the teacher tell the child not to steal and give her some extra attention. Although this logical approach had worked with other cases, it didn't work here. (We have not yet used Reality Therapy in the schools long enough to learn very much about techniques.) The teacher had tried attention and praise on many occasions, but the more she gave the child, the more she stole to gain further attention. Additional discussion revealed that everything the class could suggest had been tried and, as the class mulled it over, the problem seemed insoluble.

The class was ready to give up and send the child to the school counselor, but even this had been done. The child had been given an intelligence test, which is the regular counseling procedure in Ellen's elementary school, and found to be of good intelligence. Although it is apparent that determining the intelligence of a child who steals has no real relationship to her problem, in this situation the counselor is not allowed to do anything more.

Finally someone suggested that perhaps the teacher could get the child's attention and confidence and get her to stop stealing by telling the whole class a story about a little girl who stole. Giving the little girl the same name, Ellen, as the child who stole. the teacher would say that Ellen was unhappy, that Ellen was always upsetting the teacher and the class, and that everyone would love Ellen much more if she would stop stealing. Ellen listened very attentively.

Shortly after the story was told, she reduced her stealing and improved her other behavior. The child felt enough involved so that ceasing to act irresponsibly became worthwhile to her. The teacher was advised to repeat the story with various current embellishments until the child realized that she could get more attention and affection from the teacher by not stealing. In about six weeks the stealing stopped. During the rest of the semester Ellen's behavior and school work showed steady improvement so that it was not necessary for the teacher to tell the story any more for her; she did, however, use the same technique successfully with other children who presented problems.

The teacher was now able to become more involved with the child for all the good things she could do. She praised her for her good behavior and as the child was no longer stealing, the praise was valid. During the next semester, Ellen's performance was excellent. Because her intelligence was being put to good use to fulfill her needs, she no longer had to steal to try to do so in an irresponsible way. Although it is not clear why this particular storytelling technique works so well, it does follow the principle of presenting reality to the child—evidently in a way that he can appreciate. We have learned as the classes continue that we are always able to arrive at some approach that will work once a teacher understands and puts into use the three basic principles of Reality Therapy.

Besides teaching the class at U.C.L.A., I have been speaking to groups of administrators, school psychologists, counselors, and teachers in single sessions and one-day institutes. Following these sessions, and particularly in areas where a few follow-up sessions have been held, some teachers, administrators, and counselors have been able to put Reality Therapy to use in their work. By myself, however, I can reach only a limited number of people. A more organized method of teaching these ideas to interested school personnel is needed.

One suggestion is to train a group of school psychologists and counselors in the use of Reality Therapy. They could then work with individual schools or groups of schools in their districts. As we have discovered in Building 206 and at Ventura, the beneficial effects of Reality Therapy are increased when the whole staff works toward the same goal. Although a teacher who learns the principles of Reality Therapy from my course at U.C.L.A. and applies them by herself in a school can have some success, the cumulative effect of a whole school using these principles will be much greater in reducing the number of irresponsible children who will need more intensive care later on.

Personnel of many school districts in California have written to me expressing interest in learning to use the principles of Reality Therapy. They are not frightened of psychiatry when the concept of mental illness is not necessary and when their efforts can be successful without years of professional training. School personnel can be trained at low cost as a part of their regular continuing education. As the program starts to work, fewer children will need specialized attention. Not only will many children be helped to better lives, much money will be saved as well. It costs $500 a year to keep a child in public school, $4,500 a year for the same child at Ventura. If 10 per cent of the approximately 2,500 children in the California Youth Authority can be prevented from requiring commitment to the Youth Authority, 1 million dollars could be saved each year besides a great deal of human misery. Through the use of Reality Therapy in the public schools, mental hygiene can be extended to children when they are receptive to learning responsibility, and in a place where they feel comfortable and natural in their efforts to gain a better life for themselves.

This brief but important discussion of the application of Reality Therapy to mental hygiene concludes the book. More will be written as people begin to use the principles of Reality Therapy and add their findings to our small beginning. If we have provoked new thoughts and criticism, we welcome it; the problem of helping people to lead responsible lives will never be solved without the critical thinking of intelligent people both inside and outside psychiatry.

ABOUT THE AUTHOR

On the basis of his first book, *Mental Health or Mental Illness?* (Harper, 1961), Dr. William Glasser was invited to participate as one of a hundred leaders in all phases of American intellectual life in the Second Corning Conference, on the "Individual in the Modern World." The Corning Conferences are sponsored by the American Council of Learned Societies and the Corning Glass Works Foundation, and the second conference was held in May 1961.

Dr. Glasser has given many talks on the West Coast and in Canada and has had articles published on Reality Therapy, which he and some other doctors have been practicing for several years.

William Glasser was born in 1925 in Cleveland, Ohio, where he attended Cleveland Heights High School, Case Institute of Technology, and Western Reserve University School of Medicine. A chemical engineer at nineteen, he became a clinical psychologist at twenty-three, and a physician at twenty-eight. After medical school he received his psychiatric training at the Veterans Administration Center and UCLA. He is now a practicing psychiatrist in Los Angeles and also teaches and consults in the California Youth Authority on its program for rehabilitating delinquent adolescents. He is also associated with the Ventura School for Girls and the Los Angeles Orthopaedic Hospital. Dr. Glasser is married and has three children. His hobbies are water skiing and sailing.

◼ Perennial

Books by William Glasser:

CHOICE THEORY
ISBN 0-06-093014-4
Dr. Glasser offers a non-controlling psychology to help sustain relationships.

THE LANGUAGE OF CHOICE THEORY
ISBN 0-06-095323-3
Real-life conversations. On the left-hand page is a typical controlling order or threat, and on the right a more reasonable version, using choice theory.

CHOICE THEORY IN THE CLASSROOM
ISBN 0-06-095287-3
Glasser puts his successful choice theory to work in our schools.

REALITY THERAPY
ISBN 0-06-090414-3
Glasser examines his alternative to Freudian psychoanalytic procedures, explains the procedure, and contrasts it to conventional treatment.

CONTROL THEORY IN THE PRACTICE OF REALITY THERAPY
ISBN 0-06-096400-6
A collection of case studies and examples of Control Theory in Reality Therapy.

THE CONTROL THEORY MANAGER
ISBN 0-887-30719-1 (HarperBusiness)
Glasser explains what quality is and what managers need to do to achieve it.

THE QUALITY SCHOOL
ISBN 0-06-095286-5
An examination of coercive management in schools as an educational problem.

THE QUALITY SCHOOL TEACHER
ISBN 0-06-095285-7
Glasser shows how to establish warm, totally noncoercive relationships with students, teach only useful material, and promote student self-evaluation.

SCHOOLS WITHOUT FAILURE
ISBN 0-06-090421-6
Dr. Glasser offers daring recommendations to shake up educators.

POSITIVE ADDICTION
ISBN 0-06-091249-9
Glasser shows how to gain strength and self-esteem through positive behavior.

Available wherever books are sold, or call 1-800-331-3761 to order.